VICTORIAN LADY TRAVELLERS

VICTORIAN LADY TRAVELLERS

by

DOROTHY MIDDLETON

Academy
Chicago

Academy Chicago
425 N. Michigan Ave.
Chicago, IL 60611

Library of Congress Cataloging in Publication Data

Middleton, Dorothy.
    Victorian lady travellers.
    Reprint. Originally published: 1st ed. New York: Dutton, 1965.
With new introd.
        Bibliography: p.
        Includes index.
        1. Travelers, Women—United States—Biography. 2. Travelers,
Women—England—Biography. 3.Voyages and travels. I. Title.
CT3203.M5   1982   910'.88042 [B]   82-16353
ISBN 0-89733-062-5
ISBN 0-89733-063-3 (pbk.)

In loving memory of
SYDNEY ELIZABETH BUTLER
who told me to write this book
a long time ago

Contents

PREFACE   *page* xi

PART ONE: WELL-QUALIFIED LADIES   1

PART TWO: THE GLOBE TROTTERESSES

I. ISABELLA BIRD BISHOP, 1831–1904   19
II. MARIANNE NORTH, 1830–1890   54

PART THREE: THE CHAMPIONS

III. FANNY BULLOCK WORKMAN, 1859–1925   75
IV. MAY FRENCH SHELDON, 1848–1936   90

PART FOUR: THE SERVERS

V. ANNIE TAYLOR, 1855–?   107
VI. KATE MARSDEN, 1859–1931   128

PART FIVE: THE VOYAGER

VII. MARY KINGSLEY, 1862–1900   149

BIBLIOGRAPHY   177
INDEX   179

vii

Illustrations

1. Isabella Bird Bishop at the time of her marriage in
   1881   *facing page*   50

2. Marianne North at her easel (*Photo by courtesy
   of the Director, Royal Botanic Gardens, Kew*)   51

   Isabella Bird Bishop with her camera   51

3. North Gallery, Kew (*Crown copyright: reproduced
   with the permission of the Controller of Her
   Majesty's Stationery Office and of the Royal
   Botanic Gardens, Kew.*)   66

   Marianne North as a young woman (*Photo by
   courtesy of Mr. Roger North*)   66

4. Fanny Bullock Workman sight-seeing in Mysore
   and exploring Siachen, the Rose Glacier   67

5. May French Sheldon takes the lead in Africa   82

   Fanny Bullock Workman displays a placard   82

6. Fanny Bullock Workman and her 'trusty rover'   83

   May French Sheldon afloat on Lake Chala   83

7. Fanny Bullock Workman in a crevasse   98

   May French Sheldon in a palanquin   98

8. The Workmans in 1910   99

   Bébé Bwana pays a state visit   99

9. Kate Marsden en route for Siberia in 1890 and
   presented at Court in 1906   114

10. Annie Taylor's Pontso and his wife Shigju   115

    Mary Kingsley's friends, the Fans   115

Illustrations

11. Annie Taylor and Pontso   *facing page*   130

    Mary Kingsley's canoe on the Ogowe (*Photo by
    courtesy of The Mansell Collection*)   130

12. Annie Taylor   131

    Mary Kingsley in 1895 (*Photo by courtesy of The
    Mansell Collection*)   131

*All photographs, except where stated otherwise, are from
books by or about the travellers they portray.*

Preface

THE idea of this book first took shape in my mind over ten years ago when Mr. J. G. Murray asked me to look through some letters written by Isabella Bird on her travels, the raw material of books published by John Murray in the 1870's and 1880's. I meant to follow up the article I wrote on Isabella in the *Cornhill Magazine* (Winter 1952–3) by either a full-scale biography or by a book about woman travellers in general. Other employments supervened, but I kept up my interest in the subject and was ready for a revival of the idea when Mr. Selwyn Powell, in the summer of 1961, asked me to write a series of articles on women who travelled in Victorian times, to be published in the *Geographical Magazine* of which he was then Editor. Mr. Powell's own suggestion of Fanny Bullock Workman to begin the series of 'The Lady Pioneers' led me to choose my other subjects from among Fanny's contemporaries and this, of course, included Isabella Bird. The turn of the century proved to be an ideal period and to offer more subjects than could be included in one book. Articles on Fanny Bullock Workman, Isabella Bird Bishop, Kate Marsden, Mary Kingsley, May French Sheldon and Marianne North appeared in the *Magazine* for December 1961 and for January, March, May, June and December 1962; these, with the *Cornhill* article on Isabella, form the basis of the present book and to them I have added Annie Taylor.

My first thanks are due to Mr. Powell for having launched me on so agreeable a project, and to the staff of the *Magazine* for having reproduced the series so attractively and for their help in making available the illustrations used in this book. I am also most grateful to Mr. Colin Franklin of Routledge and Kegan Paul for suggesting that I should write the book, and for his encouragement and advice while it was in preparation. I should like to thank Mr. Murray, too, for originally introducing me to Isabella Bird and for agreeing to the use I have made now of my original researches. Access to unpublished material has enabled me to study Isabella more in depth than was possible with the others, which accounts for the perhaps disproportionate length of her chapter.

I have received much assistance in my researches from a number of people and organizations. I should like to thank both Mr. L. P. Kirwan, Director and Secretary of the Royal Geographical Society, for allowing me to make use of the Society's archives, and my friends and colleagues in the Library and Map Room for their kind co-operation in finding me books and maps and advising me on geographical points. Mr. G. Creighton of the Permanent Committee on Geographical Names gave me valuable assistance in identifying Chinese and Tibetan place-names in the chapter on Annie Taylor, and Mr. T. S. Blakeney, of the Mount Everest Foundation Trust, helped me with problems of Himalayan topography in that on Fanny Bullock Workman. I should like particularly to mention Mr. G. S. Holland who advised me on and drew the map. Much of the background to the stories was built up from material in the Fawcett Library, and both the Secretary of the Fawcett Society and the Librarian, Miss Douie, have been unfailingly helpful, and indeed inspired in some of their suggestions for research. Mrs. Rose Louise Greaves and Mr. Peter Fleming, whose books provided valuable background for Isabella Bird Bishop and for Annie Taylor, have given me useful pointers for further research, and so has Lt. Colonel F. M. Bailey who was able to throw some light on the later years of Annie Taylor. An application to the British Leprosy Relief Association for information about Kate Marsden resulted in my getting into touch with Professor N. Torsuev of Donetsk, U.S.S.R. I am most grateful to the Association's Medical Secretary, Dr. Ross Innes, for this and also to Professor Torsuev himself whose prompt and helpful reply to my letter contained details sought in vain elsewhere and which were kindly translated for me by Mr. David Balfour. I have been most kindly received at the China Inland Mission, the Prince of Wales's General Hospital, Tottenham, and the

Preface

Edmonton Public Library, and by the Director of Kew Gardens, who gave facilities for photographing Marianne North's paintings in the North Gallery. Mr. Roger North also generously made available sketches and pictures in his possession at Rougham Hall in Norfolk.

DOROTHY MIDDLETON

INTRODUCTION

In the seventeen years since *Victorian Lady Travellers* was first published, the subject has been taken up with increasing enthusiasm both in Great Britain and (even more so) in the United States. My book, based largely on the writings of the ladies themselves, seems to have set a fashion and to have opened a door into the past for a generation eager to trace the roots from which spring today's feminist movements. My travellers are seen by many as blazing a trail for the Women's Liberation movement; they provide a subject for doctoral theses; their motives are questioned and their attitudes analysed with a modern lack of inhibition they would have deplored.

New facts have come to light, some significant, some merely amusing, but none that in any way alter my original view of the subject. It is now known, for instance, that Mary Kingsley was born only a few days after her parents were married, and that the marriage was not a happy one. Her lonely childhood and a later distrust of personal relationships is therefore more readily accounted for than when I wrote my book. More has been revealed about the feuds and rivalries in Isabella Bird's Rocky Mountain paradise. May French Sheldon's adventures did not end with the century. She travelled in the Congo and in Liberia in the early 1900s, taking many photographs which have unfortunately not survived. One of these is said to have shown, when developed, the ghostly outlines of two bodies hanging in a tree, identifiable as victims of atrocities in the Congo Free State. In old age, May lived surrounded by momentos of her many activities including a brass bear used as a doorstop, given her by the Czar of Russia—but how, where, why and when is not recorded. What is more, my seven studies have encouraged research into adventures such as Alexandra David-Neel's in Tibet and Florence Dixie's in Patagonia. Here and there an explorer's wife steps out now from behind her husband's shadow to make her own contribution; the homely Mary Livingstone, for one, and the glamorous Florence Baker for another.

All this activity has extended the field and provided valuable background detail to a picture, unchanged in essentials, of individual women rejecting the stifling conventions of their time. Taking advantage of such liberating inventions as the train and the steamship, they sought freedom abroad, self-fulfilment their common purpose. Of course their objects varied widely. May French Sheldon was indeed a competitive feminist; Mary Kingsley, a seeker after knowledge, opposed even so mild an advance for her sex as election to the Royal Geographical Society. Marianne North liked to paint flowers and was unmoved by such social injustices as the prevalence of slavery in Brazil; Kate Marsden risked her life to bring help to sufferers from leprosy in remotest Siberia. Nevertheless all and many like them were at one (whether they admitted it or not) in a desire to be a person in their own right, untrammelled by domestic duties and the subordinate station accepted by so many women (especially those who were single) in Victorian society.

Dorothy Middleton,
Chelsea, 1982

PART ONE

Well-Qualified Ladies

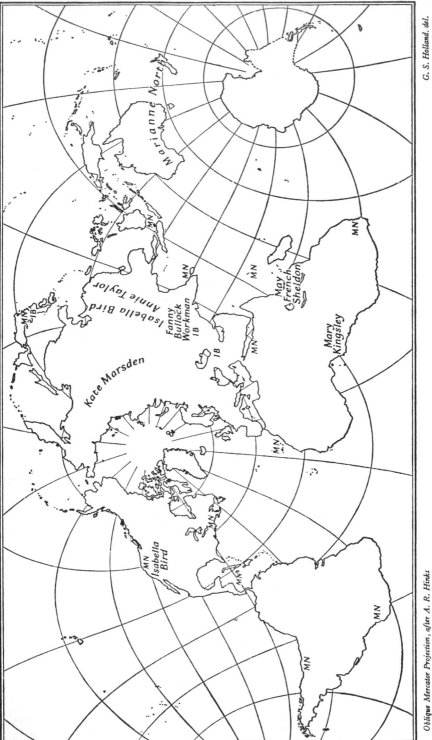

Oblique Mercator Projection, after A. R. Hinks

G. S. Holland. del.

THE WORLD EXPLORED BY SOME VICTORIAN LADY TRAVELLERS

Mrs. Dexter pitied me heartily for it made her quite ill to look down the cabin hatch; but I convinced her that no inconveniences are legitimate subjects for sympathy which are endured in pursuit of pleasure.

Six months in the Sandwich Isles, ISABELLA BIRD

TO say one is writing a book about Victorian woman travellers courts the reply: 'Lady Hester Stanhope I expect, and of course Gertrude Bell?' An early nineteenth-century eccentric and a twentieth-century scholar, these notable ladies are outside the scope of a study which seeks to describe the impulses which sent on their travels a surprisingly large number of women in the latter part of Queen Victoria's reign. From about 1870 onwards more women than ever before or perhaps since undertook journeys to remote and savage countries; travelling as individuals, and for a variety of reasons, they were mostly middle-aged and often in poor health, their moral and intellectual standards were extremely high and they left behind them a formidable array of travel books. Nearly always they went alone, blazing no trail and setting no fashion, their solitary ventures altogether different in kind from, for instance, the all-woman expeditions to the Himalaya in recent years. Though this outburst of female energy is undoubtedly linked with the increasingly vigorous movement for women's political and social emancipation, it was neither an imitation nor a development of the male fashion for exploration which was such a feature of Victorian times. Whereas the famous lone travellers among the men were followed up by expeditions of ever-greater size and complexity, the women did not inspire such an outcome. The camaraderie of the camp, so nostalgically enjoyed by the Polar explorer and the mountaineer, was not what the women were after, and played no part in the plans of such staunch contenders for women's rights as Fanny Bullock

Workman (who took her husband along) or May French Sheldon (who left her's at Naples, but dedicated her book to him). On the whole discovery has not been woman's province.

Travel was an individual gesture of the house-bound, man-dominated Victorian woman. Trained from birth to an almost impossible ideal of womanly submission and self-discipline, of obligation to class and devotion to religion, she had need of an emotional as well as of an intellectual outlet. This she found, often late in life, in travel, and though her dignity never wavered, and she seems to have imposed her severe moral standards on the very rough company in which she often found herself, she was able to enjoy a freedom of action unthinkable at home. Fortified by a kind of innocent valour, convinced of the civilizing mission of woman, clothed in long skirts and armed with an umbrella or sunshade according to the climate, the nineteenth-century woman traveller covered thousands of miles—writing, painting, observing, botanizing, missionizing, collecting and, latterly, photographing. They deplored the occasional necessity of riding astride and could rarely bring themselves to wear trousers. Although the exigencies of travel forced them into many odd conveyances—litters, carts, stage-coaches, coal-boats, the backs of coolies, elephant howdahs and even a Bath chair on wheels—they were likely to jib at a London bus on return home. Marianne North allowed herself to be persuaded by Miss Gordon Cumming to ride on one of those dangerous vehicles, but was glad to find it was going the wrong way and that they had an excuse to alight and hail a cab.

They were not, with the notable exception of Mary Kingsley, very interested in politics; many of them, but by no means all, were conventionally religious; on the whole, they accepted class and colour as they found them, and were uniformly polite, considerate and condescending to servants and savages. Considering the inadequate education of most Victorian girls, it is surprising how hard they worked at collecting information. They were particularly strong on botany and ventured rather daringly into anthropology. Observant of people and wild life rather than of places, they did not concern themselves much with the lie of the land, and there are no notable topographers among them. Their archaeology took the form of painstaking measurements, and of description rather than of explanation

4

of the temples and monuments they visited. It is almost as if they feared it was wrong to travel for pleasure, and that to bring back note-books of statistics and pages of drawings was necessary to justify the frivolity of bicycling across Java or living among the Hairy Ainu of Japan.

Today, when encyclopaedias proliferate and the more we know about things the less we seem to know about people, there are times when the books of the lady travellers seem over-weighted with instruction. 'I am something like the famous Doge at the Court of Louis XIV,' observed Mary Crawford in *Mansfield Park*, 'and may declare that I see no wonder in this shrubbery equal to seeing myself in it.' If only there were fewer Fanny Prices among our travellers, earnestly discoursing on horticulture and offering moral reflections, and more Mary Crawfords! If only they would tell us more about the wonder of themselves in the shrubbery and less about the actual trees, their books would be even more enthralling than they are. Mrs. Alec-Tweedie, a handsome, courageous young widow— one of the first professional travel-book writers—could have given many more delightful pictures of herself and her friends rattling 'through Finland in carts' if she had not been so anxious to explain the political and social position of women in the Scandinavian countries. Miss Gordon Cumming's books are, alas, almost unreadable, so informative are they. Mary Kingsley had the right idea when she crammed the 'fish and fetish' of West Africa into appendices and allowed us to enjoy her splendid narrative and sparkling anecdotes untrammelled by information. Even in Mary's case there are things we should like to know. How did they stand up physically, for instance, to the rigours of travel—they were none of them young, and the ill health so often mentioned by their biographers could not have been entirely imaginary. Isabella's letters, though not her books, hint at symptoms unconnected with her chronically weak back; Mary Kingsley had headaches and Marianne North was dogged through her life by a definite and familiar pain, apparently induced by cold weather. The hardships undergone by Kate Marsden brought on 'an internal malady'. The con-temporary male traveller is more explicit and gives some idea of what it meant to be dependent on a small medicine chest in lands without doctor or chemist. Livingstone, the rough Scots doctor, describes his ailments fairly freely and had some drastic home-brewed remedies for them. Francis Galton cheerfully recommends a charge of gunpowder in warm water or soap-suds as an effective emetic. It would also be interesting to know how they financed their trips; in default of any information on the point, one guesses at 'private means' and certainly both Mrs. Workman and Mrs. Sheldon were wealthy women. Marianne North, too, must have been left well off when her father's death left her free to journey round the world. Mary Kingsley travelled very rough, attempting to make ends meet by trading with the Congo tribes whose habits she was studying. And like other travellers before and since they counted on selling their books; probably Isabella Bird did well at this. One is left with the feeling that although primarily duty and often affection kept a number of women at home with their parents or elderly relatives, they were also prevented from breaking out by lack of money. Coming into their patrimony, Miss Duncan, for instance, and other dutiful daughters and nieces, decided to spend their small income on travel.

The Victorian passion for 'improvement'—of oneself and others—found an outlet in travel, as did their preoccupation with the far horizons where missionary, trader and imperialist alike sought fulfilment, and to cross the water was a natural idea to all classes of the island race. Emigration was a favourite solution for the social ills of the period: what scope for the 'honest poor' mused Livingstone, viewing complacently the empty uplands of Nyasaland. Isabella Bird's earliest journeys overseas were to settle into their new Canadian homes the Mull crofters she had persuaded to better their lot by going to the New World, and Marianne North took one of her more un-comfortable journeys across North America to call on some old family servants who had sought their fortune in the west. And it was not only the 'poor' who might be benefited in this way: the founding of the Female Middle Class Emigration Society in 1862 opened the door for girls belonging to the professional classes who, during the latter part of the nineteenth century, went to New Zealand and Australia, Canada and South Africa as governesses and school teachers. To convert the heathen was also a recurrent motive. Annie Taylor went to China as a missionary and there had a call to make her way to forbidden

Lhasa to save the souls of the Tibetans. Kate Marsden took upon herself the plight of the lepers of north-eastern Siberia. Mary Kingsley, an agnostic, went to West Africa to seek knowledge and returned dedicated to an imperial mission. Fundamentally, however, the strongest impetus was the growing desire of the nineteenth-century woman for independence and opportunity, a desire which crystallized in the great movements for women's emancipation and the fight for women's suffrage. Some of the travellers were more consciously influenced in this way than others. Fanny Bullock Workman was photographed on a Himalayan pass with a Votes for Women placard, and Mrs. French Sheldon embarked on her African safari, Stanley-style, in a frank spirit of 'anything you can do, I can do better'.

In the 80's and 90's women were learning to bicycle and to climb mountains. It was beginning to be possible to travel alone by train and even to make up parties to go on riding or walking holidays. *Hints to lady travellers* by Lilias Campbell Davidson, published in 1889, gives an enlightening picture not only of what adventures were coming within the reach of the supposedly weaker sex, but also of the restrictions from which they were emerging. 'Nowadays,' declares the foreword to this brisk and sensible little book, 'when a hundred women travel to one who ventured from the security of her own roof-tree in bygone days, some practical hints upon the wide subject of wanderings abroad may be useful and welcome to those whose experiences are less varied than those of their sisters.' Readers are instructed how to buy a railway ticket, and told that lady's maids are 'a great nuisance' on a journey. They are assured that membership of the Cyclists' Touring Club need not involve being acquainted with every 'adventurous youth whom they may encounter awheel', but they are encouraged to converse with fellow diners at a *table d'hôte*. 'Necessaries of travel' included a filter, a railway key and a travelling bath, and a tin of Keating's powder 'should never be omitted'. But it is the hints on packing with 'liberal use of tissue paper', each gown in a tray to itself and a monogrammed wrap for each pair of shoes, which bring home to one the emancipation of Mary Kingsley striding aboard her Liverpool cargo boat with one portmanteau, a black bag and a waterproof sack of boots, books and blankets, or of Isabella Bird with her luggage in a roll on the back of her saddle. (But the ball-dress embroidered with rhinestones and the blonde wig in which May French Sheldon astonished the African chiefs on the way to Kilimanjaro must have taken some packing, not to mention the ceremonial sword which completed the outfit.)

Indeed, it is when we come to clothes that our travellers appear at their most remarkable. The high-necked blouses and long skirts covered, we may be sure, underclothing very little different from what they wore at home. Mary Kingsley had to insist on walking behind her male companion on a jungle path because she knew the black bootlace with which she had been obliged to do up her stays was showing through her white blouse in the pouring rain. Constance Larymore, who joined her husband in Nigeria in 1902, made a little gentle fun of an acquaintance who clung to her merino combinations in a temperature of 90°F, but gave an absolute ruling on stays: '*Always* wear corsets, even for a tête-à-tête home dinner on the warmest evenings; there is something about their absence almost as demoralizing as hair in curling-pins.' Their prejudice against trousers (which even the men tended to disguise by euphemisms such as 'inexpressibles') was very strong. Mary Kingsley, forthright and original as she was, an arch-enemy of humbug, would rather have 'mounted a public scaffold' than have clothed her 'earthward extremities' in these garments, and she even went so far as to insist that a skirt was more suitable for jungle travel. When *The Times* described Isabella Bird as riding in the Rockies in 'male habiliments' she told John Murray that as she had neither father nor brother to defend her reputation, she expected him personally to horsewhip the *Times* correspondent. The lady climbers evolved, however, a daring contrivance of rings threaded with a string by which the skirt could be pulled up during difficult ascents. One of them even went so far as to suggest a riding skirt which could be discarded when out of sight of the populace and put in a rucksack. The famous Mrs. Le Blond once remembered, when in sight of home, that she had discarded her skirt only too thoroughly in a hut on the far side of the mountain over which she had come, and felt obliged to go all the way back for it. Tolerance of trousers did, however, gain ground. Miss Mené

Muriel Dowie captivated the delegates to Section E of the British Association at Leeds in 1890 when she stood up to read a paper on her recent tour of the Carpathians, *The Queen* described her as 'a tall girlish figure in a tasteful brown costume, with puffed-up sleeves and adorned with handsome lace, with a smart little hat perched on her head'; it was certainly 'difficult for her hearers to realize the appearance which she must have presented while on her travels. To use her own language, having in those far off hills no fear of Hyde Park before her eyes, she shed her skirt and bestrode her pony in all the glory of knickerbockers; and, when tired of riding, she took off her sandals and walked the mountains barefoot.' A show of bicycling clothes in 1895 ranged from 'the boldest of knickerbockers to the quietest of skirts'; and these knickerbockers were even recommended by a fashion writer in *The Queen* in preference to a divided skirt, though of course they were for country wear only. Lilias Campbell Davidson would not have approved of all this, for when she advised ladies climbing mountains to have their skirts as short as possible she meant they were 'to clear the ankles', but drew the line 'at the modern feminine costume for mountaineering and deer-stalking, where the skirt is a mere polite apology—an inch or two below the knee, and the result hardly consistent with a high ideal of womanhood'.

A high ideal of womanhood—that, behind all the impulses and desires which sent the ladies travelling, was the image they sought to maintain. The men in the rough cabins and cargo ships swore less when there was a woman in the company (or, as they preferred to describe themselves, 'an English lady'), the name of Britain glowed brighter, the Queen they all honoured was better served. If any generalization is possible about so diverse a band, it is that they did not travel to find romance— not the romance, that is, of a love affair. The emergence of woman as a being in her own right seems to have been accompanied by a certain Puritanism which repudiated the harem conception, an idea only thinly veiled by the poet's high sounding 'He for God only, she for God in him'. Mrs. Alec-Tweedie, who had been very happily married, and was the mother of two fine sons, rather unfairly alludes to 'the animalism of husbands' in one of the passages of advice to women and girls with which her books are so heavily overweighted. Isabella Bird's star-crossed love affair with Rocky Mountain Jim strikes an incongruous note. It is true it only comes to light because her letters are available as well as her published work, and that even if our other ladies had had love affairs they would not have told the public about them. Nevertheless, it is impossible to read the unselfconscious accounts of journeys alone with a man, or as the only woman in a miners' camp or Wild West saloon and to imagine that sexual adventures were in their minds at all. They were often pressed by well-meaning gentleman acquaintances to carry a revolver (presumably to protect their honour) but there is never any record of their having to use it, nor did they want to be encumbered with fire-arms. Their letters abounded in assurances to home-keeping friends and relations of the perfect safety with which a lady could travel among cannibal Africans, primitive Japanese and (probably more dangerous) the wild men of the American frontier. Nor was ordinary companionship the good they sought in their rambles. There was more than enough of this in the comfortable middle-class homes from which they came. Marianne North maintained that the only time her plans went wrong was when she travelled with a companion. Miss Duncan and Miss Christie, meeting in a valley of Ladakh, greeted each other in friendliest fashion, then pitched their tents as far apart as possible, and agreed to strike camp on different days in order to avoid travelling together. This was in perfect accordance with the views of the travelling sisterhood; they loved their relations and friends but they loved also to escape, to be themselves under foreign skies with no personal demands and obligatory duties—heaven forbid that a devoted sister should join them in the South Seas or the affairs of a favourite niece detain them in London!

The Royal Geographical Society, without whose accolade no Victorian traveller could be said to have arrived, was slow in acknowledging the claims of women. In 1847 'it was not deemed expedient at present' to consider a suggestion that ladies should be admitted as Fellows. In 1860 the Patron's Gold Medal was awarded to Lady Franklin whose persistence in sending a series of expeditions in search of her husband, presumed lost in the Arctic, had resulted in such enlargement of geographical knowledge as to amount to the discovery of the long-sought North-west Passage. In 1869 Mary Somerville, then in her ninetieth year, received the Patron's Medal in recognition of her services to geographical education, and as a belated salute to her standard work *Physical geography*, published in 1848. Neither of these ladies received her medal in person, and the awards accorded no status to women as a whole. It is, perhaps, interesting to note in passing that only five women in all have been thus honoured by the Society since its foundation in 1830. When John Hanning Speke returned from Africa in 1860 full of enthusiasm for the Dutch traveller Alexine Tinné who had been up the Bahr-el-Gazal branch of the Nile, his proposal to have her created an honorary member was not taken up.

The Jubilee of Queen Victoria in 1887 underlined the curious fact that a woman might be honoured as Patron of a Society to which women were not admitted as members, and in 1892 the Council daringly invited a female traveller to address a meeting. The formidable Mrs. Bird Bishop had, as Isabella Bird, been exploring the continents of the world for some twenty years, and was a valued member of the Royal Scottish Geographical Society which had admitted women since its foundation in 1884. She had just returned from the East, was something of a lioness, and had her answer ready: she had already been invited to address the Scottish Society, which she considered had the first claim on her, and was giving a lecture to its London branch, recently established on the doorstep of the R.G.S. The brilliantly successful meeting with the Duke of Argyll in the chair which heard Mrs. Bishop's account of Tibet was the last held by the Scots in London. Seriously alarmed by the success of its rival the R.G.S. threw open its meetings to members of all other British geographical societies, and thus found itself admitting women through, as it were, the back door. Clearly the position was absurd; at the Council meeting of 4 July 1892 the President proposed Mrs. Bird Bishop as a Fellow, and the Council unanimously agreed to the election of women on the same footing as men. The decision was published in the *Proceedings* for August, and on 28 November 1892 fifteen 'well-qualified ladies' were elected arranged in alphabetical order, the first on the list to be welcomed and introduced by the long-disused formula: 'In the name and by the authority of the Royal Geographical Society I hereby declare you a Fellow thereof.' Fittingly, Isabella Bird Bishop headed the list but in her absence abroad the ceremonial welcome was received by Miss Maria Eleanor Vere Cust whose father, Mr. R. N. Cust, a distinguished Orientalist, was a zealous advocate for the admission of women as Fellows. Miss Cust, who acted for many years as her father's secretary, and also worked as a missionary in India, only died in 1958 when she had reached the age of ninety-five.

Facing the general meeting of the Society with the *fait accompli* of these elections, the Council was shaken to its august roots to find challenged, by a group of dissentient Fellows, its competence to elect to the Society anyone it thought fit. Officially the objection was on legal grounds—did the Council's admitted right to elect Fellows without reference to a general meeting include the right of electing women? The Council insisted that there was nothing in the Society's Charter to preclude women as Fellows, and that the pronouns 'he' and 'his' in the by-laws were a convenient way of indicating all classes of 'Her Majesty's loving subjects', and not specifically men. (True, a reference to 'gentlemen' in the Library's regulations was less easy to explain away, but regulations were not by-laws.) The Council supported their claim, furthermore, by quoting such sister societies as the Royal Statistical, whose first lady member, Miss Florence Nightingale, had been elected in the ordinary way in 1858, the Zoological who had had women as members for sixty years, and the Royal Asiatic which, as a Fellow remarked during a later meeting, had 'an exceedingly able and learned lady as Assistant Secretary'.

The dissentients were led by Admiral Sir Leopold McClintock, who had been Jane Franklin's choice as leader of the expedition which, nearly forty years before, had finally established the fate of Sir John Franklin and the men of the *Erebus* and *Terror*. The end of the search, and the priority of Franklin's discovery of the North-west Passage, was marked in 1860 by the presentation to Lady Franklin of the Patron's Gold Medal and to McClintock of the Founder's. The Admiral nevertheless declared now that 'although admission of ladies might make the Society more or less enjoyable, I do not think it would intensify the geographical character of it'. Admiral

Halliday Cave put the case more cogently from the legal standpoint, but the argument degenerated pretty rapidly from a high-minded challenge of the autocratic Council into a wrangle over the suitability of women to belong to the Society and (more alarming) to be admitted to the direction of its affairs.

Throughout, the controversy generates that flavour of 'The Ladies! God bless 'em!' so typical of assemblies of Englishmen when called upon to take women seriously. Were the ladies to be beautiful or scientific, enquired one Fellow archly, while another deplored the probable decline of their Learned Society into a Garden Party Society. One speaker was reproved for referring to women rather than to ladies. Another hoped to defer their admission for 100 years. A Fellow in favour of their election reassured the doubters as to the possibility of any question coming up for discussion 'which would make the presence of ladies undesirable'. In any case, there need be no fear that any one would propose electing a lady to the Council for 'a very long time'—the British Association for the Advancement of Science had not done such a thing in fifty years. Admiral Inglefield agreed to election with restrictions; Admiral Cave (the sea-dogs were in full cry) had already gone on record as saying: 'I should be very sorry to see this ancient Society governed by ladies.' So potent has been the influence of the ghosts of the Franklin Search, that not until 1933 was a woman first elected to the Council of the R.G.S. when the well-known traveller Mrs. Patrick Ness took her place at the table. Women are still not elegible to join the Geographical Club which entertains speakers before evening meetings.

A Special General Meeting of the Society (packed by the dissentients) voted against the ladies; a referendum to the whole Fellowship gave clear approval of their election without restriction. Learned Counsel were consulted by both sides, and correspondence columns of *The Times* seethed. George Nathaniel Curzon, just back from his travels in Asia, was violently opposed to the admission of women: 'Their sex and training render them equally unfitted for exploration, and the genus of professional female globe-trotters with which America has lately familiarized us is one of the horrors of the latter end of the nineteenth century.' An unhappy compromise was arrived at: the election of women was to cease, but the twenty-two who had meanwhile become Fellows might remain. *Punch*, and a good many others, including the Society's Secretary Douglas Freshfield, who resigned, saw the controversy as ludicrous and its solution as absurd.

A lady an explorer? A traveller in skirts?
    The notion's just a trifle too seraphic:
Let them stay and mind the babies, or hem our ragged shirts;
    But they mustn't, can't, and shan't be geographic.

And still the salts are fuming, and still the ladies sit,
    Though their presence makes these tars, who women trounce, ill.

For no woman, bless her petticoats, will ever budge a bit,
    Having once been made a Fellow by the Council.

Punch was quite right; far from budging, Miss Marsden presumed so far as to apply for a ticket to the Annual Dinner in 1894, but was refused on the grounds that she would be 'the only lady among 200, nearly all of them smoking'. Not that Kate Marsden, recently returned from riding through the forests of north-east Siberia with an escort of Cossack soldiers, would have been unduly incommoded by this.

Twenty years later, in 1913, under the Presidency of a converted Lord Curzon, the subject was raised again. A referendum gave a 3 to 1 vote in favour of electing women (as compared with 2.5 to 1 in 1893), the opinion of Learned Counsel was again taken, a Special General Meeting adopted the proposal, and the Lyceum Club gave a dinner to celebrate one more victory for common sense.

Of the twenty-two ladies elected during 1892 and 1893, only three have left sufficient record behind them to find a place in the pages that follow. Marianne North was too early, Mary Kingsley and Fanny Bullock Workman too late to qualify, but Kate Marsden and May French Sheldon took pride in their right to put F.R.G.S. after their names, Mrs. Sheldon going so far as to inscribe it herself in the British Museum copies of her books. Isabella Bird Bishop expressed some disgust at the Society's shilly-shallying and was particularly offended at Curzon's discourteous references to woman travellers, for she had met him, and thought they were on friendly terms, during her Turkish and Persian journeys. Nevertheless, she was sufficiently gratified by her election to keep in close and active touch with the Society. The *Journal* in the 90's printed several communications from her about her progress in the Far East, and in May 1897 she delivered a full-scale lecture to the Society on her journeys in Szechwan, the only woman to address them until 1905 when Fanny Bullock Workman spoke on her travels in the Himalaya. She joined, too, in discussions at meetings addressed by men, and was always regarded with great respect. These accounts of some of the 'well-qualified ladies' are based almost entirely on their published work and are not intended as definitive portraits. It was not my intention, even if it had been within my capacity, to analyse the political theories of Mary Kingsley or to give a history of Himalayan exploration at the time the Workmans were claiming their records. Most of the women described here led full and busy lives at home as well as abroad of which I have made little or no mention. They appear here simply as travellers, the guise in which they are most interesting to me and, I venture to think, are most themselves. It is, of course, easy to be amusing about them, to chuckle at Fanny Bullock Workman in a crevasse and at May French Sheldon in a palanquin—indeed, they often make fun of themselves. But when the laughter dies away one is left with nothing but admiration for their vitality and their fortitude. One is caught up, too, in that happiest of human emotions—unaffected delight in the visible beauties of the world. The engaging Jane Ellen Duncan, crowded out of this book by her more strenuous and better documented sisters, speaks for most of them in her *Summer Ride through Western Tibet*.

At sea-level the pressure of the air on the square inch is 15·22 pounds; at 18,000 feet, a little higher than the Chang La, it is 7·66 pounds, and this reduction brings on headache, dizziness, and bleeding at the nose and ears in many cases, while if the heart is at all weak the consequences may be very serious . . . but in my case I felt the air so exhilarating that I could have laughed and sung from pure joy, if there had been any one to keep me in countenance, and I was in the saddle for seven and a half hours continuously that day without feeling tired . . . I gave this account of crossing the Chang La to a literary friend to read, and his criticism was that I did not harp sufficiently on the agonies of the journey; but as I did not suffer any agonies, I do not quite see how the harping is to be done. At the time it seemed throughout an easy, commonplace affair which anybody could have accomplished, and I have no gift of fine writing to cast a glamour over it and make it seem the tremendous achievement it was not.

Isabella Bird in her '*thoroughly serviceable and feminine costume for mountaineering and other rough travelling*'.

PART TWO

The Globe Trotteresses

I

Isabella Bird Bishop
1831–1904

The Stars are setting and the Caravan
Starts for the Dawn of Nothing—Oh make haste!
Rubaiyat of Omar Khayyam, TRANSL. E. FITZGERALD.

1. ISABELLA BIRD

'THREE globe trotteresses all at once!' It was not a greeting to
endear the enthusiastic 'Lady Λ.' either to Marianne North,
who tells the story, nor to Miss Constance Gordon Cumming
standing 'with her great hand on my shoulder' while they were
presented to Isabella Bird Bishop in whose honour the party
was being held. 'We retreated as fast as we could' writes Miss
North tartly, 'leaving Miss Bird unruffled and equal to the
occasion.'

The year was 1882, and the picture of Isabella at the height
of her fame provides as good an introduction as any to the most
dramatic of Victorian lady travellers. 'She was seated in the
back drawing-room in a big armchair, with gold-embroidered
slippers, and a footstool to show them on, a petticoat all over
gold and silver Japanese embroidered wheels, and a ribbon
and order across her shoulders, given her by the King of the
Sandwich Islands. She was being interviewed in regular Yankee
fashion, and I was taken up to her the moment I came in.'
Thus Miss North, who had expected someone very fragile and
small, but found instead 'a very solid and substantial little
person, short but broad, very decided and measured in her
way of talking, rather as if she were reciting from one of her
books'.

Isabella Bird was not everyone's favourite, inspiring in about equal proportions admiration, exasperation and that kind of idolatry which women of vigorous personality command from their less strong-minded sisters. Her emotions were violent, her health precarious and her energy phenomenal. She possessed a cast-iron digestion for food as for facts and sights, covering thousands of miles on horseback over the highest mountain passes and in native boats down the farthest rivers of the world, on a handful of rice and raisins, her mind, eye and ear agog for the wonders of nature and (for she was of her time) for improving information and moral lessons. When she said 'I do not care for any waterfall but Niagara,' she summarized once and for all her passion for the sublimities of Nature, which she was to seek in all quarters of the globe for the best part of thirty years: volcanoes in eruption, hurricanes howling 'in one protracted, gigantic scream', the romantic snows of the Rocky Mountains and the desolate uplands of Asia—such experiences aroused to rapture this high-minded and intellectual Victorian lady with a Clapham Sect background and perpetual ill-health.

Isabella Lucy Bird was born on 15 October 1831, at Boroughbridge, Yorkshire, of a prosperous middle-class family with a powerful tradition of service to God and the community. Her grandparents were first cousins, and she was related to William Wilberforce, whose influence was strong in old Mr. Bird's house at Taplow. Here members of the Clapham Sect were frequent visitors, and Isabella had early recollections of the long Evangelical Church services which made her back ache. Aunt Mary Bird was a missionary in India, Aunt Henrietta had refused a clerical suitor on a doctrinal scruple and pined away; Aunts Rebecca and Catherine took their tea without sugar long after the Emancipation of the West Indian slaves had deprived this gesture of its poignancy. Her father, Edward Bird, had turned his back on a wordly career at the Calcutta Bar to take orders when he was over thirty, and had married Dora Lawson, a clergyman's daughter with a genius for teaching which she exercised in her husband's Sunday school and to the benefit of her two daughters.

Isabella's key to freedom from this duty-bound world was put into her hand at a very early age when the doctors recommended that the sickly and fretful child should live as much out of doors as possible, and she went riding with her father round his Cheshire parish—she (then under ten) on one carriage horse and he on the other. This was typical of the upbringing of the Bird girls, for there were no concession to childishness in that household; no baby books or fanciful answers to questions were allowed, and the children learnt from the beginning to ride a big horse, to read the whole Bible, to comprehend the full truth of every subject. When Mr. Bird, high-minded and impulsive, moved the family from rural Cheshire to labour in the murky vineyard of Birmingham, Isabella was barely in her teens; but she taught in her father's Sunday school and helped to bear the obloquy which his zeal for temperance and Sunday observance brought upon the family. Finally, after a breakdown in health, Mr. Bird accepted the living of Wyton in Huntingdonshire (near Cowper's Olney), where he died in 1858. Her father, Isabella declared, had been the mainspring of her life, and indeed they were much akin, the able and enquiring mind hampered in each by nerves too easily disordered. Henrietta Bird seems to have resembled her mother, and it was upon these two affectionate but undemonstrative women, with their strong intellectual interests and deep piety, that Isabella now focused her turbulent emotions.

Mrs. Bird and her daughters went to live in Edinburgh, and when her mother died in 1866 Isabella concentrated her affection even more fiercely on her sister; but when Henrietta decided to make her home at Tobermory Isabella's devotion did not extend to living with her in what she declared was an unendurable climate. The physique which was to withstand the icy winds of the Persian uplands, the enervating heat of Malaya, the drenching rains of Hawaii, broke down at the mere contemplation of actually living in the Isle of Mull; living, moreover under the shadow of a younger sister whom the islanders had adopted as a kind of local saint. She was now at a climacteric of her life; the constant backache, the insomnia and nervous fears to which she was a martyr, grew worse and worse, and a complete collapse seemed inevitable. In truth the frustrated egosim which is a part of all strong natures was struggling to be free and could not find release within the range of a Victorian woman.

The doctors prescribed a change of scene and in the July of

1872 Isabella left for Australia on a tour designed to last eighteen months. She did not linger in the Antipodes and New Year's Day, 1873, saw her embarked on a vessel of rumoured unseaworthiness bound out of Auckland for the Sandwich Islands. At last Isabella Bird had found herself: a hurricane smote the rickety *Nevada*, the stewards went on strike and there was an invalid *in extremis* on board. Isabella enjoyed it all; she wrote to her sister describing the voyage as 'very pleasant', thanks to the 'moral, mental and social qualities' of her fellow passengers. She got out her sewing, helped to nurse poor young Mr. Dexter and read *The Idylls of the King*—in between whiles she joined heartily in killing cockroaches with a slipper and in playing quoits. She stayed in the Sandwich Islands for six months where she saw much of the missionaries and was careful to investigate the religious life of the natives; she shook her head over their easygoing habits, but the pagan within her, the lover of light and beauty and the open air, blossomed and flowered. How she loved it! Among other things, she recovered her joy in riding. Her spine had become so painful that she had given up her favourite exercise, but when she saw that European as well as native women rode astride in this happy land where it was always afternoon, she determined to see if it would suit her better than the conventional side-saddle. Like most of her fellow Victorian travellers, Isabella had strong views about women's civilizing mission and a horror of 'masculinity'; at first she feared to be so untrue to her sex as to ride 'cavalier fashion', but she was persuaded to do so and it proved the easiest, the safest, the most enjoyable pursuit imaginable. On the comfortable peaked Mexican saddle, wearing a 'dainty bloomer costume' in 'Macgregor flannel' she set out to explore the Hawaiian Archipelago with a thoroughness which alarmed her friends and caused her enemies to accuse her of exaggeration and of spinning travellers' tales. She rode up volcanoes, through gulches where she was nearly drowned by water in spate and across the green open country accompanied by admiring, carefree natives crying '*Paniola! Paniola!*' When she asked what the word meant 'Mrs. Rice said, "Oh, lassoing cattle, and all that kind of thing." ' Isabella was disposed to accept the inference as a compliment; 'but when I told Mrs. R. that the word had been applied to myself, she laughed very much, and said she would have toned down its meaning had she known that!' Her health improved and long letters in fine writing on thin paper poured into the cottage at Tobermory describing the delights of solitary camping, assuring Henrietta that a lady could travel with 'perfect security' in the islands; she stayed with natives in their huts and she scrambled to the top of several volcanoes, where the eruptions filled her with ecstasy. Her heart had been set on ascending Mauna Loa, and when a certain Mr. Green asked her to come up with him to see what promised to be a fine show of fireworks, she accepted at once. Miss Bird frequently rode off into the blue with a male companion like this, and no one, least of all herself, seems to have thought it improper. She got on well with men and rather preferred them to her own sex. When the journeying mood was on her, she thought of nothing but getting there, and was totally unembarrassed by the intimacies of travel—a native servant in Japan, an administrative officer in Malaya or India, a cowboy in America, a missionary in China, it was all one provided they helped her to arrive at her goal and made the time pass with their conversation; her emotions were fully occupied with the strange sights and sounds of nature, and quite unengaged by her companion. On this occasion, she and Mr. Green shared a tiny tent on the brink of Mauna Loa's vast crater with their native guides, and when the fleas woke her in the night she crawled unconcernedly over the sleeping bodies of the men to get out of the tent and watch the flames. 'Circumstances were singular', she observed to Henrietta, referring merely to the discomfort and strangeness of sleeping on ridges of lava within sound of the 'roar, clash and thunder of the mightiest volcano in the world'.

The excitement and edification she derived from her volcanoes were varied by cosy visits to the homes of settlers and missionaries, by studies of the native people in their own homes, by inspections of schools and leper settlements, and attendance at church. Henrietta was so impressed by the success of the cure that she wrote suggesting she might come out and join her sister. The transports came to an abrupt end: 'I shall be in the Rocky Mountains before you receive my hastily-written reply to your proposal to come out here for a year,' she wrote from Honolulu on 6 August 1873, 'But I will add a few reasons against it, in addition to the one which I gave regarding the benefit which I now hope to derive from a change to a more stimulating climate.' Henrietta had, indeed, strangely mistaken her part—the passive vocation of the Pole to which the needle must point or the mariner be for ever lost. The relationship was an odd one, almost as if Henrietta was another self to whom Isabella must communicate her every experience or be but half a person. And how to communicate an experience which they shared? Henrietta would have been as much *de trop* in Hilo as Isabella (one suspects) felt herself at Tobermory. After Henrietta's death in 1880, Isabella encompassed many interesting and important journeys, but she never again wrote about them so attractively. Her letters are couched in passionately affectionate terms; 'My Own Pet' is her favourite opening, sometimes 'My Ownest', and ending 'Its Own Pet.' Sometimes, when she had not received an expected letter, she would write in desperate strain, and sign herself, 'Its Poor Pet.' Little invented words are scattered over the pages: 'dil', for instance, means dull and inactive. Often she would reassure her sister by writing boldly along the top of the page: 'Nothing Annoying in This'; any emotional difficulties were 'annoying'—an admirer in Honolulu is described as having 'quite, unannoying ways' but one is left with the feeling that she enjoyed a rather more animated manner in her friends, even if at the time it 'annoyed' her. Henrietta kept these letters, and they form the basis of the books which John Murray published for Isabella with profit and pleasure to all concerned. Mr. Murray became a great friend—she deferred to his opinion in most things, was introduced to Mr. Gladstone by him, asked him to help her choose a tricycle, and expected him to defend her when she was misrepresented in the Press.

In July 1873, still dutifully in pursuit of health, Isabella Bird left Honolulu for San Francisco, and on 2 September she wrote to Henrietta from the solitary beauty of Lake Tahoe in Nevada where the stillness was only broken by the sound of a woodman's axe. The pure mountain air of Colorado was said to be good for invalids, and Isabella decided to go there, to try and lodge with some settler's family and to see something of the Rocky Mountain country. She had brought from Hawaii a riding dress consisting of 'a half-fitting jacket, a skirt reaching to the ankles, and full Turkish trousers gathered into frills which fall over the boots—a thoroughly serviceable and feminine costume for mountaineering and other rough travelling in any part of the world'. Her first mountain ride went very well, apart from a toss taken when her horse shied at a grizzly bear, and the man who hired a mount was not at all shocked at her riding 'cavalier fashion'. Nevertheless, she was prepared to throw her leg over the peak of the Mexican saddle and 'ride sidewise' in populated districts, bearing in mind the harm done by women in uncivilized parts of the world 'by noisy self-assertion, masculinity, or fastness'. Her fury was extreme when *The Times* later reported her as having worn 'masculine habiliments' during her tour of the Rockies.

From Cheyenne, by horse or wagon as opportunity offered, Miss Bird went south-west towards the eastern foot-hills of the Rockies. She meant to get into Estes Park, one of the famous open spaces in the Rockies, just under Long's Peak, and which is now part of the Rocky Mountains National Park. She arrived at the end of September in the dusty little town of Longmount, stewing in the setting sun, with flies everywhere, but with a glorious view of the sun setting over the Rockies, ten miles distant. The landlord, a jovial, kindly man, declared it would be 'a real shame' not to see Estes Park, and if she did not mind the cold and could 'ride horseback and lope' he could get her an escort for tomorrow. Two young men (described by the landlord as 'innocent'—Miss Bird sought in vain while in their company to discover what this meant) were going up to the park and would show her the way, and he would hire her a horse. Doubtful of her capacity for the venture, apprehensive of her health, Isabella nevertheless closed with the offer at once, and her next letter was written ecstatically from 'Estes Park! ! !'

Estes Park is some thirty miles from Longmount and is reached easily enough today by one of Colorado's State Highways. But for Isabella there was only a devious track through the green cottonwoods and golden aspens, running at first through the picturesque canyon of the St. Vrain, and rising up to 9,000 feet where a cleft in the hills opened out into McGinnis Gulch; here the trail broadened between grass verges on which tall pines grew. She had been riding for ten hours before she reached the summit and saw the lovely upland valley lying a few hundred feet below her, the setting sun bright on the Thomson River and on Long's Peak. For once, Henrietta was too distant an audience—she must share the moment with someone who would understand, and looking round she saw a rough cabin which promised human company. A collie lay at the door, a beautiful little Arab mare grazed near by, and a man emerged, shaggy enough for a bear but with something gracious in his manner. 'Broad and thickset,' she described him after this first of many meetings, 'about the middle height, with an old cap on his head, and wearing a grey hunting suit much the worse for wear . . . a digger's scarf knotted round his waist, a knife in his belt, and a "bosom friend", a revolver, sticking out of the breast pocket of his coat; his feet, which were very small, were bare, except for some dilapidated moccasins made of horse hide.'

Jim Nugent, known as 'Rocky Mountain Jim', was an Irishman born in Canada who had run away from home as a boy. After a series of adventures, including a spell with the Hudson's Bay Company, he came south to the United States in the old heroic days of frontier expansion and took service with the Government as a scout, escorting emigrants across the plains and waging war with hostile Indians. His prowess against the Redskins and his skill as a pioneer were legendary in his own day, but 'the fame of his many daring exploits' was 'sullied by crimes'; he drank like a fish, was subject to ugly and dangerous moods, and was morbidly superstitious. On the other hand, he was well-read, intelligent, quick-witted, generous in a dramatic kind of way and had, when he chose, the manners of a courtier. He was proud of his record and flattered by frequent references to himself in the local Press; he liked to talk of the days when he rode into town in his scout's uniform with its red sash, his hair falling in sixteen golden curls on his collar, and the girls running wild for him. A predatory way with women was not, however, one of Jim's vices; his reputation for chivalry and the respect in which he held 'good women' were well known in the territory, and he was one of those shaggy characters of whom children are instinctively fond. He was about forty when Isabella met him, and she found him immediately attractive—'such an agreeable facility of speech!'—but was never quite sure how far she was merely dazzled by his charm, nor to what extent the good balanced the bad in his nature. He was a handsome man, now marred by his untidy appearance and by the scars on his face where a bear had clawed him—'one eye was entirely gone, and the loss made one side of the face repulsive, while the other might have been modelled in marble' noticed Isabella, fascinated by the deep-set blue of the other eye, the fine aquiline nose and the well-shaped mouth. She was surprised when this wreck of a man, lifting his tattered cap, asked her in a pleasant Irish voice what he could do for her. Clearly he was a gentleman, and likely to be better company than the 'innocent' young men whom she had rather heartlessly left far behind, She asked him for a drink of water, which he brought her in a tin can, and the romance of her life began.

Isabella galloped the last mile of her journey at full speed and drew up hungry, excited and happy, at a neat cabin by the side of a small lake. Around the cabin were corrals for cattle and all the apparatus and outbuildings of a farm. A cheerful-looking man ran out to greet her and introduced himself as Griffith Evans, a Welshman from the slate quarries near Llanberis who, with his partner Edwards, owned the ranch with its 1,000 head of cattle roaming in the park. The Evans and Edwards families formed the nucleus of a small settlement where visitors, come into the mountains for sport or for reason of health, could be put up during the summer. Isabella was at once offered a comfortable little cabin for as long as she liked to stay, although it was late in the year and the women and children were preparing to go down to Denver for the winter.

She was at home at once in the 'joviality' of the Estes Park settlement. The fine air revived her; eager to lose no time while the weather held she was determined to get to the summit of Long's Peak (14,000 feet above sea-level) and to make a tour of the district with Estes Park as her base. Mountain Jim offered to act as guide up the peak, and with the two 'innocent' young men, they set off early in October to make the ascent. They carried the minimum of equipment and food for the three-day journey, but even so Isabella was loaded up with three pairs of blankets and a quilt which reached to her

shoulders on the back of the Mexican saddle, from the horn of
which hung a pair of Evans's boots, borrowed for the climb.
Jim turned out looking like a ragamuffin, teasing his horse to
display her paces to the lady, but such was the grace of his
manner and so agreeable the flow of his conversation, that
Isabella soon forgot his appearance and forgave his showing off.
The three hours' ride passed in a flash. Miss Bird and Mr.
Nugent were, in fact, well launched into the delightful border-
land between friendship and love where time is scarcely long
enough for the exploration of personalities and the enjoyment
of confidence. The ride, she wrote to Henrietta, was 'one series
of glories and surprises, of "park" and glade, of lake and stream,
of mountains on mountains, culminating in the rent pinnacles
of Long's Peak, which looked yet grander and ghastlier as we
crossed an attendant mountain 11,000 feet high'.

They camped at the timber-line, a big half-moon beaming
out while the afterglow of sunset lingered, gilding the eternal
snow on the flanks of Long's Peak. The two young men had
'little idea of showing even ordinary civilities', but Isabella had
been told she would find Jim a gentleman if she treated him
as such, and so she did, addressing him always as 'Mr. Nugent'.
She assured Henrietta that although his manner was 'bolder
and freer than that of a gentleman generally, no imaginary
fault could be found'. He ordered his dog Ring to stay by her
and the faithful beast went immediately to lie with his head in
her lap gazing all the while at his master. Gathered round the
fire, the little party sang a few songs, and then listened to
Jim's Red Indian stories and to 'a very clever poem of his own
composition'. When Isabella retired to a 'luxurious bed' of
pine-needles, with a saddle for a pillow, she lay awake, not in
pain or distress of mind as so often at home, but in an exaltation
of spirit which made nothing of the wolves howling beyond the
shadows or of the bitter cold. Ring lay at her back and in the
dying glow of the fire 'it was strange to see the notorious
desperado, a red-handed man, sleeping quietly as innocence
sleeps. But above all, it was exciting to lie there, with no better
shelter than a bower of pines, on a mountain 11,000 feet high,
in the very heart of the Rocky Range, under twelve degrees
of frost, hearing sounds of wolves, with shivering stars looking
through the fragrant canopy, with arrowy pines for bed-

posts, and for a night lamp the red flames of a camp fire.'

The 3,000-foot ascent of Long's Peak next day was an ordeal she would always remeinber; her fatigue and giddiness were such that she would never have reached the top 'had not "Jim" *nolens volens* dragged me along with patience and skill . . . which never failed'. The young men, who hinted that a lady was rather an impediment on such a trip were soundly snubbed and left to their own devices. Once at the summit, Isabella was visited by the same glorious feeling of isolation as she had felt at Mauna Loa, of being 'uplifted above love and hate, and storms of passion', standing as she was on the backbone of America.

The descent was nearly as painful as the journey up. 'Jim' was unfailingly kind, bringing her at last (the young men in unregarded attendance) to their camp of the night before. She slept soundly in her arbour of pines, waking to a bright moon and with feet so cold she came to the fire and sat there the rest of the night, the beloved stars of her homeland a shining pledge of stability overhead—the Plough and the steadfast Pole Star, the glittering Pleiades, and great Orion sprawled over the cold, dark sky. Thus armoured in thoughts of home and in her own integrity, she listened through the northern night to Jim's melodious voice telling her, with tears on his cheeks, of the tragedy of his life, and of how 'a great sorrow' in youth had driven him to a lawless life. 'Was it semiconscious acting?' she wondered, 'Or was his dark soul really stirred to its depths by the silence, the beauty, and the memories of his youth?'

Isabella's next letter was dated some days later, and written in tearing spirits. The shy, pious, little lady of Edinburgh, too busy with her studies and her charities for any social life, and too ill for amusement, was transformed into the popular 'Miss B.' whom Griff Evans would wake at sunrise with a cheery thump on the door as he cried: 'Will you help drive in the cattle? You can take your pick of the horses. I want another hand.' And very well she did it, as well as any man, the cowboys told her, as she galloped across the sward, in and out of the ravines, rounding up the cattle through ten hours of the crisp autumn day. On Sundays she loved to be left alone with her Bible and prayer-book to worship in 'the temple not made with hands,' undistracted by the 'back view of bonnets'. In the evenings, the logs piled high in the wide fireplace, Evans led the singing in 'John Peel' or 'Rule Britannia', or the dour, teetotal Edwards might be induced to tell stories of his march through Georgia with Sherman. Sometimes one of the English tourists, up in Estes Park for the elk hunting, dashed off strathspeys on the harmonium, and Isabella wrote her letters to the noisy wheezing music or to the strains of a mouth organ played by a young French-Canadian. The men always had a joke for her when the time came for her to say good night and to seek her lonely cabin across the grass down by the lake, and there were roars of laughter at her discovery of a skunk which had a lair beneath her floorboards and which no one dared disturb.

Beneath the harmony of the little group lurked danger, of which Isabella soon became aware; 'Mountain Jim', brooding on his dark past in the cabin in McGinnis Gulch, was at odds with popular, cheerful, peppery Evans—both men drank, Griff for sociability and Jim in bitter silence, and quarrels were frequent. But during that carefree October, things were easier; Jim had no ugly fits, and day after day Isabella's heart warmed to see the little Arab mare tied by the main cabin while Jim came to call. 'It is so sad you can never see me as I am now,' she wrote to Henrietta, 'with an unconstrained manner, and an up-to-anything, free-legged air.' So up-to-anything did she prove herself, caring for the horses, washing the dishes, baking the bread, telling stories, that Evans asked her to stay for the winter at 6 dollars a week to look after him and Edwards after the women went down to Denver, where Mrs. Evans was to lie-in. It would mean too much baking, she told him jovially, she would rather ride after the cattle; and in any case she could delay no longer if she was going to make the tour she had promised herself and see something of the country.

On 20 October, despite the imminence of winter, heralded by a heavy snow-storm in the park, Isabella set off on Birdie— a bay Indian pony 'with legs of iron, fast enduring, gentle and wise; and with luggage for some weeks, including a black silk dress' strapped behind her saddle. Jim met her to say good-bye on the Longmount trail; looking wild, as usual, but fascinating her by his 'gentle, cosy manner', as he leant for a minute on her horse and said: 'I'm so happy to have met you. So very happy—God bless you', and she rode on gaily, escorted by the musical French-Canadian, who looked after her most carefully—'I do like a gentleman who always knows the right thing to do and say.'

The ride from Longmount to Denver was long and dull, thirty miles of featureless prairie with only an occasional herd of lean Texan cattle, a solitary horseman with rifle over his knees, or a covered wagon labouring along the barely discernible trail, to break the monotony. She had been told to 'steer south, and keep to the best beaten track', and so she rode alone all day, and raced the gathering storm until, coming to a brow of the prairie in the late afternoon, she looked down upon Denver, 'the great City of the Plains, the metropolis of the Territories'. Mrs. Evans and the children welcomed her warmly and she lost no time in mapping her route for what she called her ravage in the Rockies. Birdie was to be her only transport and, independent and completely mobile, she planned to make south for Colorado Springs and to come back through the foot-hills. This would show her such famous places as the Great Gorge of the Manitou and the fantastic rock formations grouped in the Garden of the Gods, and if the weather held on the high ground, she meant to ride up westward and to stand on the Great Divide.

In the twenty years or so since the territories of America's far West had been opened up, Denver had developed into a respectable city, 'a shooting affray is as rare as in Liverpool, and one no longer sees men dangling to the lamp-posts when one looks out in the morning! It is a busy place, an entrepôt and distributing point for an immense district, with good shops, some factories, fair hotels, and the usual deformities and refinements of civilization.' Isabella was impressed by the large number of saloons, by the wild-looking characters lounging around who probably found the restraints of civilization as irksome as she did the obligation to ride 'sidewise' through the capital. She studied the masculine crowds which thronged the streets—huntsmen and trappers; men of the plains with belts and revolvers; teamsters in leather suits; horsemen with hairy buffalo hide boots; Broadway dandies in kid gloves; English tourists, supercilious yet comely; inscrutable Indians on their tiny ponies; here, she knew, was where men like Mountain Jim, Buffalo Bill and the rest came to spend the money they made trapping and hunting, to paint the town red, to show off before the few women who had come so far into the wilderness.

She rode south towards Great Platte Canyon, in and out of creeks, ravines and canyons, putting up at ranch or settlement as occasion offered or compelled. At one rough cabin the roost was ruled by a fierce woman who smoked a clay pipe which she handed round the family; at another she melted the suspicions of some dour pioneers by peeling potatoes and making scones. For the most part, she was made cheerfully welcome, the women exclaiming at her frailty and her amazing courage; the men, she observed, generally assumed she was as strong as themselves. One night she came through a snow-storm to a millionaire's ranch with hot water laid on and a staff of negro servants; once she stayed in a boarding house where a poor young consumptive had lately died, and sat in the kitchen from where she could see the dead man's feet, ghastly and immobile, sticking out from the bedclothes. She rode into Colorado Springs, 150 miles from Denver, a week after leaving the capital, draped in a long skirt and with her leg thrown over the saddle-horn: 'a queer, embryo-looking place,' she thought it, 'yet rising, and likely to rise'. She rode up through the Ute Pass among Colorado's most exotic scenery—strangely-coloured rocks and great gorges all around her. On 1 November with winter bearing down on the mountains she rode north-west and still upward towards the Great Divide of the Rockies, through tracts of forest, masking who could tell what wild beast ready to spring out of the shadows? A group of men at one of her ports of call spent the evening arguing about the best way up to the Divide, and agreed that it was the worst road in the Rocky Mountains, likely now to be thick in snow. She found the way, however, riding across the northern tip of the mining area of South Park and up the Breckleridge Pass. Her way was beguiled by a picturesque stranger met on the road, Comanche Bill, who was one of Colorado's famous characters and compared favourably with Isabella's own desperado in Estes Park by being so very well turned out. His hair (can Miss Bird have been exaggerating?) hung in curls nearly to his waist, he wore a beaded buckskin suit and large brass spurs and was provided with an arsenal of weapons. Comanche Bill's parents had been killed in a massacre years before at Spirit Lake, his sister had disappeared and he had been seeking her ever since, slaying every Indian he saw, in revenge. To Miss Bird, his manner was 'frank and respectful' as he showed her the watershed of the Rockies, where snow trickled down east towards the Platte and the Atlantic, and west into the Colorado and Pacific; bidding her a courteous farewell, he went on his way while she turned back for the Denver road. She stumbled that night into a tipsy party at Hall's Gulch, and was greeted by a man in the 'good-natured and sapient stage of drunkenness'. Whisky, she wrote to Henrietta, was the curse of the West; ordinary crime hardly existed, doors were never locked and property safe, a woman might ride anywhere alone (Isabella always assured her sister that this was so in whatever outlandish part of the world she was travelling). But whisky led to murder, and to every kind of degradation. Hall's Gulch was the only place where she had seriously bethought her of the pistol Jim had insisted on her carrying and which she found an intolerable encumbrance.

She returned to Longmount by way of Golden City and Boulder, and there decided to go back to Estes Park where she could live without ready cash until Evans repaid the money she had lent him in an emergency before she came away. It did not, after all, seem a very hard fate to go back to her 'grand solitary, uplifted, sublime, remote, beast-haunted lair'. There was some mutual dismay when Isabella arrived after riding alone from Longmount and being greeted by Jim at the top of the pass. At the ranch were only two young men, Kavanagh and Buchanan, who had been hunting in the park and had agreed to care-take until the return of Evans and Edwards from Denver in what they hoped would be a few days' time: actually, it was a whole month before the owners reappeared—long enough for Isabella to become involved in a difficult emotional situation from which she longed to retreat into Henrietta's impersonal calm, just as she was accustomed to retreat from her devotion to Henrietta by departing on her travels. She and the two young men settled down happily together; the men brought in wood and water and the lady washed up and put the rooms to rights, an old shawl for a

tablecloth and a comfortable store of tea in the cupboard. But
things were not so easily settled with Jim—in the course of a
long, wild ride in a snow-storm he told her that he loved her.
He had first become aware of his feelings on Long's Peak, and
her absence had but confirmed them. Now she knew why he
had been so silent—so 'dil'—since her return, but he made up
for it now, pouring into her unwilling ears the story of his
mispent life. Much she had heard before (Jim was an Irishman
and not reticent), but some of the more disgraceful episodes
he now disclosed were new to her, and distressed her im-
measurably. Years afterwards, when Jim was dead, she declared that the things he told her that afternoon 'come between
me and the sunshine, sometimes, and I wake at night to think
of them'. Horrified, alarmed and strangely thrilled, her
dominating emotion was yet pity; she felt torn with regret that
such a lovable and fascinating man, one with 'real genius',
should so have ruined his own life. 'He is a man any woman
might love, but no sane woman would marry,' was her verdict
when she thought it over, knowing how deeply he drank and
how ungovernable was his temper. Having thoroughly distressed and frightened her, so that she was in tears and speech-
less, Jim wheeled his horse round into the falling snow and
declared as he rode off his intention of camping out on the
Range till she had gone. She tried to compose herself, but as
night fell her thoughts turned to the desperado freezing for love
of her out on the hillside.

Some days later he walked into the parlour, and asked her,
with chilly politeness, if she would care to have pointed out
to her a trail she had wanted to know about—he was off on a
long trapping excursion and if she could find her own way back
he would take her so far. No reference was made to their last
encounter, he coughed dismally throughout the ride, and dis-
played about as much animation as a corpse; when he said
good-bye to her at the parting of their ways he barely touched
her hand in farewell. Isabella was thoroughly piqued and,
thinking him out of the way, wrote him a prim and angry note
(beginning 'Dear Sir' and ending 'Yours truly, I.L.B.')
begging him to keep out of her sight for the time she was
obliged to remain in Estes Park, since his 'blameworthy'
conduct had caused such restraint between them. Riding to his

cabin, she met him on his way back looking miserably ill—an old arrow wound in his lung troubled him, he told her pathetically, and he was going to bed; it was good of her to write, he added, taking the note with mournful courtesy and putting it unread in his pocket. Poor Isabella! she rode back swiftly, her heart full of pity—she longed to bring him back with her, to 'make him warm tea and be kind to him'. Next day, the play-acting came to an end between them. On an impulse, Isabella saddled Birdie and galloped towards the cabin in McGinnis Gulch, convinced that Jim was dying, only to meet him riding towards her with a chastened countenance and a request for 'an hour's conversation'.

They sat under a tree, their only companions Birdie and the little Arab mare, and talked quietly in the lull which mercifully succeeds great storms of emotion. He told her 'rationally and calmly' of his situation and prospects—of his squatter's claim here in the mountains, his forty head of Texan cattle and his trapping skill. He hinted wistfully that perhaps Miss Henrietta Bird might come out and join them in Estes Park; one cannot help thinking that Isabella's affection blinded her when she assured Henrietta how much she and all their friends would like him. But Isabella 'told him that if all circumstances had been favourable and I had loved him with my whole heart, I would not dare to trust my happiness to him because of whisky'. There were no histrionics that day, and although she knew that her earnest pleas to him to give up drink made little impression, they both felt happier for their talk.

Was she in love with him? 'There's a man I could have married,' she admitted later in her journal to Henrietta, and from first to last he was fascinating, lovable and her very dear friend. She liked a man who could talk well, and, what is more, Jim epitomized for her the wildness of nature to which she had given a heart no human was ever wholly to possess. Though she never again wrote with the freedom of her letters to Henrietta, one can read between the lines of her later books how, to the end of her life, she enjoyed travelling with a man who was thoroughly masculine—the 'wit and brutal frankness' but withal real kindness of Major Sawyer was to take her through the mountains of Persia sixteen years later with something of the enjoyment she had felt on Long's Peak with

'Mr. Nugent'. As for Jim, one can but guess that he admired her gallant spirit and respected her thorough goodness, untainted as it was by any trace of complacency; Isabella Bird never expected people to be any better than they were, nor claimed any extraordinary virtue for herself. And she was such good company! Despite her piety, she could make Jim laugh like a schoolboy with anecdotes of their mutual acquaintance, told with just enough malice to be funny, but never meanly. When he felt serious, she could meet him in conversation on a higher plane; his superior in knowledge of the poetry he loved, willing to be taught by him about the ways of nature and of the wild country where both were at home, there was no limit to their pleasure in each other's company. He was clever enough, too, to be amused at her not being afraid of him, or impressed by his dramatic moods. He tried her pretty high one day by firing a shot over her head as she rode down the Longmount trail in a snow-storm, and followed up this demented gesture by pulling her from her horse into his cabin, scolding her for being out on such a day. She answered him with such spirit that he burst into a roar of laughter and they sat down to drink coffee very companionably by the fire. She then rode on as she had intended wondering (not for the first time) how far Jim's moods were put on for effect. Once, it is true, she dreamt he levelled a gun at her in earnest, but even in her sleep she knew she was in no danger.

After their talk under the tree, something of the old companionship returned. She went riding with him, and once spent an afternoon in his cabin, chaperoned by Mr. Allen, a foot-loose young student who had turned up at the ranch, where he ate more than his share. She had written an account of the ascent of Long's Peak for the Denver magazine *Out West* and had brought it to Jim to criticize; forgetting, in a self-absorption typical of her, that their unlucky love had sprung into being on that expedition. She felt strangely at home in the squalor of the trapper's hut: they talked of poetry and spiritualism and she read her article aloud to him, while Mr. Allen (who had literary pretensions) listened unregarded. But she knew things could not last thus; though she was 'howling fearfully' (one of her little expressions when writing to Henrietta) at the idea of leaving Estes Park, there was sense in the Scots proverb 'Better a finger off than aye wagging'. Jim's temper was worsening, and when the party at the cabin invited him on 25 November to a Thanksgiving Day dinner, he refused ungraciously, railing at life's injustices in a difficult meeting she had with him among the bones and hides round his dismal hut. But Evans and Edwards returned at last, Isabella's loan was repaid, and when Jim offered to ride with her to the plains and bring back her horse there was nothing to keep her.

Her companions of the last month bade good-bye to her with real regret, wishing they could be as 'quiet and gentlemanly' as when a lady was with them. Evans rode with her to McGinnis Gulch and before she left she had the satisfaction of seeing the two men shake hands. Jim and Isabella set off, she riding his Arab mare, and making him promise he would 'neither hurry nor scold'. Talking quietly and seriously they rode all day, to spend the night with a young Mr. Miller who had the 'clear eyes and manly self-respect which the habit of total abstinence gives'. He finished the dishes in ten minutes after supper, and was ready to sit down and smoke at ease while a woman, thought Isabella, would have been fussing about till bedtime. The young settler and the desperado discussed—of all things— the best way of making bread and biscuits, and one wrote out a recipe for the other. They combined to make her comfortable for the night, heating a stone for a hot-water bottle, warming blankets and piling up the fire to combat the mercury falling to eleven below zero.

Next day they left for the last thirty miles to the stage-coach which was to take her to the railway at Cheyenne. They heard, as they began to come to houses, that there was to be a dance at the inn where they were to spend the night and, low-spirited and overwrought as they both were by now, the news alarmed them. Suppose, thought Isabella, Jim drinks and gets into a quarrel, while he confessed he had dreamt the night before that just such an incident had occurred and he had killed a man. When they got there they found that only a quiet regular gathering of neighbours was on hand and that they could stay in the kitchen and need not join in. The men came crowding to peer in at the door when they heard it was 'Rocky Mountain Jim' sitting there so quietly, with the children of the house on his knee pulling his hair. They may, too, have come to look at the lady with him, the fame of whose exploits as a horsewoman had spread through Colorado, but if so Isabella was too modest to mention it.

Eventually the dancing began, and the two strangely-assorted friends were left alone, she to write her eternal letters while he copied some poems she had brought to his notice, reading them aloud to her, 'with deep feeling'. Then she spoke to him for the last time, begging him to reform his life before it was too late. 'It might have been once,' was all he said. 'He has excellent sense for everyone but himself,' she wrote in her last letter from Colorado, 'And . . . a gentleness, propriety, and considerateness of manner surprising in any man.'

There was no lying awake that night, no nightmare of violence, only a deep and somehow happy conviction which followed her into her dreams that the parable of the one repentant sinner and the ninety-and-nine just persons was meant specially for Jim; he had told her he said his prayers and believed in God, and to God (the merciful Father of her constant imagining) she must leave him. Her last sight of him was as the coach rattled away next morning, and she watched him ride off over the snow, the sun glinting on his yellow hair. Five months later he was dead. The enmity which had smouldered so long between him and Evans burst into flame, guns were drawn, and Griff shot him down near the cabin where Isabella had lived so gaily, and where Jim used to tether his mare when he came to call. He lived long enough for Isabella to hear the news of the affray before his actual death; she declared that he came before her in her room in the Swiss hotel where she was then staying, at the very moment he breathed his last, in fulfilment of a promise they had made each other at parting. Five different versions of the quarrel were written to her, but she kept them to herself, lamenting in bitter anguish that Jim should have died as recklessly as he had lived.

In 1878 she received a proposal from Dr. John Bishop, the Birds' family doctor, a man as unlike Jim as might well be. Declaring to John Murray that she could not face being 'an invalid wife' Isabella fled to recruit her health by a trip to the Far East. In Japan she rode on native pack-horses and lived among the Hairy Ainu, the aborigines of remote Hokkaido.

Isabella Bird Bishop, 1831–1904

She grew amazingly better, studying the habits of the Ainu—
'at this moment a savage is taking a cup of *sake* by the fire'—
and assuring her sister that nothing had occurred during her
stay that 'could in any way offend the most fastidious sense of
delicacy'. From Japan she sailed for Hong Kong, and put in a
gruelling expedition to the prison and execution ground at
Canton, the grim description of which in an elegant Victorian
travel-book stands out surprisingly. John Murray, indeed,
wished to omit it from *The Golden Chersonese*, but she insisted it
was good for people to know what happened in 'the dark
places of the earth' where justice was another name for torture,
and criminals were crucified.

She went on to Malaya, landing *en route* at Saigon and taking
a long, observant walk inland from the harbour. She rather
despised Singapore where the only subject of conversation was
the arrival of the mailboat, but she enjoyed up-country Perak
where she rode on elephants and made friends with a pet
ape—'when it sits with its arms folded it looks like a gentlemanly person in a close-fitting fur suit'. She came home by way
of Egypt, her health failing as she approached journey's end.
It was three weeks after her arrival in Mull before she could
even walk into near-by Tobermory.

In 1880 Henrietta died. Prostrated with grief, Isabella at last
accepted the faithful Dr. Bishop and was married in the spring
of 1881 in deepest mourning. John Bishop was a gentle,
humorous, supremely unselfish man—he and Isabella had
first become acquainted when studying histological botany and
he regarded her with a quizzical devotion which enabled him
to say: 'I have only one formidable rival in Isabella's affections,
and that is the high tableland of Central Asia.' When asked how
so frail a lady accomplished such strenuous journeys he smiled
benignly and diagnosed: 'The appetite of a tiger and the
digestion of an ostrich.' Isabella's fervent adoration of her
husband, and her emotional dependence on him, give the lie to
a story which was going the rounds at the time when Marianne
North was annoyed by her airs—she admitted she would like
to visit New Guinea, but she was married now and it was
hardly a place you could take a man to.

2. ISABELLA BISHOP

HER husband's death after only five years of marriage was the culminating tragedy of Isabella's life, but it did not stop her travelling. Rather, her activity became compulsive and her adventures progressively more arduous, as if with the snapping of all close emotional ties she was left with no alternative but to pursue, in ever widening circles, a fulfilment which eluded her. Rationalize as she would, setting a practical goal for each journey, and assembling on her return a mass of useful information, her travels became increasingly a contest with nature and a defiance of man. Indeed, she came to have less and less value for the human element she met in so wide a variety of guises. She who had enjoyed playing with the carefree Hawaians and living with the gentle Ainu, concluded at last that 'savage life does not bear a near view. Its total lack of privacy, its rough brutality, its dirt, its undisguised greed, its unconcealed jealousies and hatreds, its falseness, its pure selfishness, and its treachery are all painful on a close inspection.' Only the sky and the hills never failed her. With every journey her immunity to cold became more complete, her appetite less fastidious and her tolerance of discomfort almost an addiction. The courage and high spirits which carried her through the winter 'ravage' in the Rockies took on an almost desperate quality on the gruelling ride across the snowbound mountains between Baghdad and Tehran. Only in China, perhaps, with its vast distances, turbulent rivers and, above all, its wide plains leading her ever up the inaccessible mountains of Tibet, did she approach what she was seeking.

Because she was high-minded and very intelligent, and because nothing destroyed an unexpectedly realistic sense of humour, she tried to give some purpose to her endless journeyings. Finding more and more comfort in religion she underwent the ordeal of baptism by total immersion at the hands of the famous Dr. Spurgeon as a gesture of dedication to missionary endeavour, and decided to visit the mission fields of the world. With this object she set sail for India early in 1889 and from there went on to Turkey and Persia; it was as a tour of Far Eastern missions that she conceived her tremendous traverses of Korea, Japan and China from 1894 to 1897. When it suited her and (one assumes) them, missionaries accompanied her on stages of her journeys and her later books contain many very sensible observations on the purpose and use of Christian missions in Moslem and Buddhist lands, and some very tame descriptions of the missions themselves. In fact, it may be doubted, good Christian though she was, whether evangelical piety was really the mainspring of her dynamic energy. The books she wrote after Henrietta's death have little of the individual sparkle which make *Six months in the Sandwich Islands*, *A lady's life in the Rocky Mountains*, *Unbeaten tracks in Japan* and *The Golden Chersonese* so delightful, but the journeys themselves are more impressive. *Journeys in Persia and Kurdistan, Korea and her neighbours* and *The Yangtze Valley and beyond*, overweighted though they are by trade statistics and moral reflections, tell a story at times hair-raising, at times drily humorous, and contain some of her finest descriptive passages. They give too some pleasant glimpses of the traveller absorbed in her work—developing photographs in the silt-laden waters of the Yangtze, falling into a ten-hour sleep in her travelling dress to awake 'clutching my interrupted diary', or 'eating my curry, as usual from a piece of millboard on my lap, with a Jaeger sheet pinned round my shoulders'. And she is a mistress of the throw-away line—'When I was sleeping in a buffalo stable in Turkey', for instance, or 'being an experienced muleteer I had to arrange the loads for each pony'.

The object of her Indian journey in 1889 was to found mission hospitals in memory of her husband and sister, and the quest for suitable sites took her into Kashmir. Bored with the social life of India's playground, she escaped on a tour of western Tibet and, mounted on a 'silver-grey Arab . . . untamable, tireless, hard, hungry', rode over the Zoji La into Ladakh and spent two months on the journey in western Tibet which earned her the belated notice of the Royal Geographical Society.

Her next project was to ride through the little-known mountain regions of Turkey and Persia visiting not only such missions as had achieved a footing in these (to Isabella) benighted Moslem lands, but also the ancient Christian communities of the Armenians, and the Nestorians of Turkish Kurdistan. Her friends were trying to dissuade her from this dangerous employment when she had the good fortune to fall in with Major Herbert Sawyer, of the Intelligence Branch of the Quartermaster's Department of the Indian Army. Major Sawyer was about to start on a geographical and military reconnaissance of south-west Persia which would take him through the Bakhtiari country and Luristan, regions Isabella was particularly anxious to visit. He agreed to let her join his caravan, in any case from Baghdad to Tehran and on to Isfahan where he himself would be taking off into the Zagros mountains. The spirited way in which she tackled the first part of the journey obviously impressed him, and they eventually joined forces for the Bakhtiari reconnaissance, Isabella providing her own supplies and servants, but enjoying the protection of Sawyer's sentries when camping in wild country.

It might be extraordinary that an old campaigner like Herbert Sawyer, who comes straight out of the pages of *Kim*, should even consider escorting a pious and middle-aged widow of reputedly frail physique on a journey through unfamiliar and probably hostile country, but there was nothing extraordinary about the journey itself. It was all part of the 'Great Game' which the Government of India had been playing for the last half-century, an elaborate under-cover campaign to thwart Russia's imperialist designs in Central Asia. Our lady travellers were often caught up in the fringes of the game: the Survey of India had been in the Karakoram long before Fanny Bullock Workman, busy at its task of forestalling Russian penetration; Annie Taylor in her Yatung shop saw Younghusband go through on his mission to save Tibet from Russia; Isabella's later books contain frequent references to Russia's sinister influence in countries as far apart as Persia and Korea. The 'Great Game' (the phase seems to have been coined sometime in the 1840's) varied in intensity according to who was in the ascendant in Whitehall and Delhi. The party of 'masterly inactivity' advocated a defensive strategy on India's frontiers, with an occasional punitive expedition to keep unruly tribesmen in order; the advocates of what the rival party called 'mischievous activity' favoured the peaceful penetration of Persia and Afghanistan (later of Tibet), buffer States which were to be persuaded to submit to British influence, to modernize their economies and reform their laws according to British advice. Major Sawyer's mission was no doubt linked with an active phase in Anglo-Persian relations which was signalled by the appointment in 1888 of the energetic Sir Henry Drummond Wolff as British Minister at Tehran. High on the programme of desirable reforms suggested to the Shah was the building of railways, and in measure as Russia seemed to encroach on Persia's northern frontier so did Great Britain press the advantage of opening up the south to British trade and international contacts through the Persian Gulf. Here the Karun river offered a navigable waterway into the interior (that interior where today lie the rich oilfields of south-west Persia), and British diplomacy scored a signal success when, in the October of 1888, the Shah agreed to open the Karun to vessels of all nations. Major Sawyer's instructions to survey the land and assess the people on the far, or north-east side of the Zagros range were obviously connected with further plans for opening up the way to Isfahan through southern Persia, and with possible development of the land by irrigation and mining schemes. It was not his first visit to Persia, for he had been detailed in 1887 to submit a report on the military value of the Russian Trans-Caspian railway, the obvious strategic nature of this line along the northern frontier causing considerable concern in Delhi and in Whitehall.

Major Sawyer was very much the kind of man Isabella liked, having a 'splendid appearance, force of character, wit, brutal frankness, ability and kind-heartedness'. They got to know each other on the ride from Baghdad to Tehran, and she acknowledged that she could never have got through without him. Either because she liked to tell her own story in her own way or because he preferred to be anonymous, he is nowhere in her book mentioned by name; he appears in *Journeys in Persia* first as M—, later as 'The Agha' (or 'Master'). They left Baghdad on 21 January and arrived at Tehran on 26 February 1890, more dead than alive after a ride which even today by car can be uncomfortable enough in winter. Snow blizzards were driving over the hills, and choking the passes so that of two caravans meeting the weaker was driven off the road into the deep drifts. As they came down to the lower ground the drenching rain turned the roads into seas of mud which were sometimes impassable. They put up sometimes at caravan-

43

serais, sometimes in village inns, and once in the local Governor's house for some days while they waited for the floods to subside, always in considerable discomfort. 'Not fit for a beast!' exclaimed Sawyer surveying Mrs. Bishop's accommodation on one occasion. *Journeys in Persia* contains several hair-raising descriptions of wayside halts of which the following is typical:

> The floor was deep with the manure of ages and piled with bales and boxes. In the side recesses, which are about the height of a mule's back, the muleteers camped with their fires and their goods, and laid the provender for their beasts in the front. These places are the mangers of the eastern caravanserai, or *khan*, or inn. Such must have been the inn at Bethlehem, and surely the first step to the humiliation of 'the death of the cross' must have been the birth in the manger amidst the crowd and horrors of such a stable.
>
> The odour was overpowering and the noise stunning, and when our wet, mud-covered baggage animals came in, adding to the din, there was hardly room to move, far less for the roll in which all mules indulge when the loads are taken off; and the crush resulted in a fight, and one mule got his fore-feet upon my 'manger' and threatened to share it with me. It was an awful place to come to after a six hours' march in rain and snow, but I slid off my mule into the recess, had it carpeted, put down my chair, hung a blanket up in front, and prepared to brave it, when the inhabitants of this room, the one place which has any pretensions to being a room in the village, were bribed by an offer of six *krans* (about four shillings) to vacate it for me. Its 'pretensions' consist in being over a gateway, and in having a door and a square hole looking on the street; a crumbling stair slippery with mud leads up to it. The roof leaks in every direction, and the slimy floor is full of pools, but it is luxury after the caravanserai stable, and with one waterproof sheet over my bed and another over myself I have fared well, though the door cannot be shut, and the rest of the party are in the stable at an impassable distance.

Some of the worst weather struck them between Kermanshah and Qum.

> It has been a severe day. It was so unpromising that a start was only decided on after many pros and cons. Through dark air small flakes of snow fell sparsely at intervals from a sky from which all light had died out. Gusts of icy wind swept down every

gorge. Huge ragged masses of cloud drifted wildly round the frowning mass of Piru. Now and then the gusts ceased, and there was an inauspicious calm.

I rode a big mule not used to the bit, very troublesome and mulish at first, but broken in an hour. A clear blink revealed the tablets, but from their great altitude the tallest of the figures only looked two feet high. There is little to see on this march even under favourable circumstances. A few villages, the ruined fort of Hassan Khan, now used as a caravanserai, on a height, the windings of Gamasiab, and a few canals crossed by brick bridges, represent its chief features. Impressions of a country received in a storm are likely to be incorrect, but they were pleasurable. Everything seemed on a grand scale: here desolate plateaus pure white, there high mountains and tremendous gorges, from which white mists were boiling up—everything was shrouded in mystery —plain prose ceased to be for some hours.

The others had to make several halts, so I left the 'light division' and rode on alone. It became dark and wild, and presently the surface of the snow began to move and to drift furiously for about a foot above the ground. The wind rose to a gale. I held my hat with one half-frozen hand. My mackintosh cape blew inside out, and struck me such a heavy blow on the eyes that for some time I could not see and had to trust to the mule. The wind rose higher; it was furious, and the drift, not only from the valley, but from the mountainsides, was higher than my head, stinging and hissing as it raced by. It was a 'blizzard', a brutal, snow-laden north-easter, carrying fine, sharp, hard-frozen snow crystals, which beat on my eyes and blinded them.

After a short experience of it my mule 'turned tail' and needed spurring to make him face it. I fought on for an hour, crossed what appeared to be a bridge, where there were a few mud hovels, and pressed on down a narrower valley. The blizzard became frightful; from every ravine gusts of storm came down, sweeping the powdery snow from the hillsides into the valley; the mountains were blotted out, the depression in the snow which erstwhile had marked the path was gone, I could not even see the mule's neck, and he was floundering in deep snow up to the girths; the hiss of the drift had increased to a roar, the violence of the storm produced breathlessness and the intense cold numbness. It was dangerous for a solitary traveller, and thinking that M— would be bothered by missing one of the party under such circumstances, I turned and waited under the lee of a ruinous mud hovel for a long, long time till the others came up—two of the men having been unhorsed in a drift.

Later, when her mule succumbed to the cold, 'M— kindly put my saddle on a powerful Kermanshah Arab. I soon found that my intense fatigue on this journey had been caused by riding mules, which have no elasticity of movement. I rode twenty miles today with ease, and could have ridden twenty more, and had several canters on the few places where the snow was well trodden.' 'I really like this journey,' she concludes cheerfully some pages later, after cataloguing a series of calamities and hardships, 'except when I am completely knocked up, or the smoke is exceptionally blinding.'

There is a friendly suggestion of her Rocky Mountain rides in the description of the last lap into Tehran. 'Abbas Khan and the sick orderly were sent on early, with a baggage mule loaded with evening dress and other necessities of civilization; the caravan was to follow at leisure, and M— and I started at ten, without attendants, expecting to reach Tehran early in the afternoon.' In fact, it took ten hours through seas of mud to reach the British Legation, where they found 'every window was lighted, light streamed from the open door, splashed carriages were dashing up and setting down people in evening dress'—the Drummond Wolffs had arranged a dinner party to welcome her and Major Sawyer. 'Caked with mud from head to foot, dripping, exhausted, nearly blind from fatigue from the mud hovels and the congenial barbarism of the desert' she could only stagger to her room and collapse on the hearthrug before the fire.

The Bakhtiari adventure began at Isfahan on 30 April and lasted a little over three months. It was, Major Sawyer records in his official report, 'very hot, and the atmosphere thievish'. He only once mentions his companion, when Mrs. Bishop was 'so threatened with upraised sticks and shouts that she had to draw her revolver'. The ride was over wild and exciting country, along and across the upper waters of the Karun and Diz rivers, the homeland of the wild Bakhtiaris and Lurs who, though Persian subjects, owed little fealty to anyone but their own Khans. They would, Isabella and the Agha thought, have welcomed annexation by Britain. Life in the Bakhtiari hills was delightfully free from 'purposeless bothers' except, perhaps, the social duty of visiting the harems of the local chiefs, whose loneliness and boredom stirred the latent Victorian feminist in

Isabella. She enjoyed her meals of 'roast mutton, rice, chapatties, tea and milk, without luxuries or variety', and used to good effect the medicine chest given her by Burroughs & Wellcome before she left England. The sick came from far and near, and as the only containers they possess were a few cooking pots, there was constant difficulty in doling out small quantities of medicine; one poor woman trotted off with her ration of eye-lotion in an eggshell:

> The tents were scarcely pitched before crowds assembled for medicine. I could get no rest, for if I shut the tent the heat was unbearable, and if I opened it there was the crowd, row behind row, the hindmost pushing the foremost in, so that it was 8 p.m. before I got any food. Yesterday morning at 6 I was awakened by people all round the tent, some shaking the curtains and calling *'Hakim! Hakim!'* and though I kept it shut till 11, and raised the mercury to 115° by doing so, there was no rest.
>
> From 11 o'clock till 9 p.m., except for one hour when I was away at the Khan's, I was 'seeing patients' wishing I was a real instead of a spurious *Hakim*, for there was so much suffering and some of it I knew not how to relieve. However, I was able (thanks to St. Mary's Hospital, London) to open three whitlows and two abscesses, and it was delightful to see the immediate relief of the sufferers. 'God is great', they all exclaimed, and the bystanders echoed, 'God is great'. I dressed five neglected bullet wounds, and sewed up a gash of doubtful origin, and with a little help from Mirza prepared eye-lotions and medicines for seventy-three people. I asked one badly-wounded man in what quarrel he had been shot, and he replied he didn't know, his Khan had told him to go and fight. . .
>
> I had been standing or kneeling for six hours, and had a racking headache, so I reluctantly shut up my medicine chest and went by invitation to call on the Khan's wives, but the whole crowd surrounded and followed me, swelling as it moved along, a man with a mare with bad eyes, which had been brought ten miles for eye-lotion, increasing the clamour by his urgency. *'Khanum! Khanum!'* (lady), *'Chashma!'* (eyes), *'Shikam!'* (stomach) were shouted on all sides, with *'Hakim! Hakim!'* The people even clutched my clothing, and hands were raised to heaven to implore blessings if I would attend to them.

At Burujird Major Sawyer turned back to Isfahan and Isabella set off alone on the long ride through Kurdistan to Trebizond. She had some bad moments when her muleteers held her up to ransom, and some good moments among the 'manly, frank, hospitable' Kurds with their 'kind and jolly women'. True, they were followers of Islam, and she endeavours, when she remembers, to disapprove of them. Especially was she concerned with their cruel persecution of the Nestorian, or Assyrian Christians, that strange remnant of ancient Christendom, who were of such burning interest to the missionizing Victorians, and through whose villages her way lay. But what halcyon days she had when riding with a wild escort in 'full Kurdish finery' shrieking, yelling, and juggling with riding sticks! And what a pet she made of her horse ('my faithful, woolly Boy'), a far more interesting character than Screw, the reliable but dull animal who had carried her over the passes and through the rivers of Luristan. It was 'Paniola' over again, transmuted into the sombre hues of her later years: for the Hawaian greensward, the dusty brown plains of Asia Minor, and for the innocent, garlanded islanders, the savage Kurdish tribesmen; only the galloping horses were the same. What a pity, she reflected, that young lady missionaries are not able to get out of doors and have a good gallop from time to time—but must stay inside learning the language and waiting for the converts who so rarely come of their own free will.

Home in Mull for the New Year of 1891, she lectured to the British Association at Cardiff in August on her Persian journey and in 1892 was taking lessons in photography in preparation for further travel. Ignoring her rheumatism, a fatty heart and a touched lung, she left for the Far East in 1894 at the age of sixty-three, for her longest and most exacting series of journeys. During the next four years she paid four visits to Korea, travelling first up the Han river crowded into a *sampan* twenty-eight feet long with two boatmen, two Chinese servants and Mr. Miller—a young missionary who 'though not an experienced traveller cheerfully made the best of everything'.

Bored by the inactivity of boat life, she hired ponies and rode north to the Treaty Port of Wonsan on one of those intractable Korean ponies she describes so vividly: 'He trudged along very steadily, unless any of his fellows came near him, when, with an evil glare in his eyes and a hyena-like yell, he rushed upon them teeth and hoof, entirely oblivious of bit and rider.' Her original distaste for Korea changed to real interest. She had lost none of her faculty of observation for things natural and political, and wrote to Mr. Murray from Seoul on 23 January 1897 that 'the fascination of being behind the scenes in an Oriental Kingdom is great, and it has been a matter of very deep interest to watch the slow unfolding of Russian policy of which the British Consul General thinks the Foreign Office is entirely unaware and will only become aware when it is too late to check it'. She had noticed a similar situation in Persia.

After visiting Mukden and going into Manchuria, and securing a glimpse of Siberia from Vladivostok, she arrived in Hong Kong early in 1895 so ill that she could not rise from her chair without help, but well enough to lecture on Korea and Tibet to packed meetings. Well enough, too, to plan an extended tour of missions which, since the founding of the China Inland Mission in 1865, had extended far inland from the original limited sphere of the Treaty Ports. The Church Missionary and London Missionary Societies, the China Inland Mission and the Presbyterians—Isabella knew them all and had some sensible and curiously detached views on their work, particularly on those concerned solely with evangelism; of medical missions she approved whole-heartedly, had taken nursing and first aid courses in London to make herself useful to them, and administered her accolade here and there in endowing hospitals in memory of her husband, her sister and her friend Miss Clayton.

Her health recruited by a summer in Japan and a further brief visit to Korea, she set out on perhaps her most interesting and certainly her most distant voyage. For almost the first time, the conventions of the English travelling lady wear thin: she wore Chinese costume (what a pity trousers were *de rigeur*, and that the conventional Chinese were outraged by her wearing a Japanese hat!), and she frankly admitted the very real danger of mixing with crowds unfriendly to foreigners. A 'very fine-looking, superior man' named Be-Dien was engaged as a servant: 'He was proud and had a bad temper,' but 'was never out of hearing of my whistle except by permission, showed great pluck, never grumbled when circumstances were adverse, and never deserted me in difficulties or even perils.'

At Ichang on the Yangtze Isabella engaged a houseboat and settled into 'a cabin the width of the boat, with a removable front, opening on the bow deck, where the sixteen boatmen rowed, smoked, ate and slept! . . . my "furniture" consisted only of a carrying-chair, in which it was very delightful to sit and watch the grandeurs and surprises of the river'; where her two missionary companions, Mr. Stevenson and Mr. Hicks, sat, she does not say. Out of a long, didactic and extremely weighty book, *The Yangtze Valley and Beyond*, lavishly illustrated with Mrs. Bishop's own photographs, may be extracted a taut and moving story. The scenery is vividly described, conforming as it did to her insatiable appetite for natural marvels and exotic effects; the virtuous monotony of life in the missions, varied as it was by periods of acute danger when anti-foreign feeling broke out, is powerfully conveyed. And the drama of the great river itself, the roar of the rapids, the clamour of the heaving, straining men as they dragged the boats up to the beat of drum and gong and the crack of bamboo whips, these make fine reading for armchair travellers. She landed at Wanhsien after seventeen days in her boat, and set off on a round journey of 900 miles into Szechwan and north-west to within range of Tibet. Her transport was a carrying-chair, from which she frequently alighted for a healthy walk, and between missions she stayed at night in squalid and often dangerous wayside inns. In one

> The walls were black and slimy with the dirt and damp of many years; the paper with which the rafters had once been covered was hanging from them in tatters, and when the candle was lit beetles, 'slaters', cockroaches and other abominable things crawled on the walls and dropped from the rafters, one pink, fleshy thing dropping upon, and putting out, the candle! . . . Between two of the bedsteads there was just space enough for my camp bed and chair without touching them. The oiled sheet was spread on the floor, and my 'furniture' upon it, and two small oiled sheets were used for covering the beds, and on these my luggage, food, and etceteras were deposited. The tripod of my camera served for a candle stand, and on it I hung my clothes and boots at night out of the way of rats . . . With absolute security from vermin, all else can be cheerfully endured. A meal of curry, rice, and tea, was not despicable, though I was conscious that my equipment and general manner of living were rougher than they had ever been before, and that I had reached 'bed-rock' to quote a telling bit of American slang . . . The travelling

Isabella Bird Bishop at the time of her marriage in 1881.
'*The most dramatic of Victorian lady travellers.*'

Marianne North at her easel.

Isabella Bird Bishop with her camera.

'The nineteenth-century woman covered thousands of miles, writing, painting, observing and, latterly, photographing.'

was without fatigue. I walked when it suited me, and for the rest might have been in an easy-chair in a drawing-room. The chair-bearers were energetic, and their 'boss', a great wag, kept them constantly laughing.

Mostly she travelled alone, sometimes the missionaries in transit from one station to another accompanied her, and more than once she was the centre of an anti-foreign riot. 'I was in my chair in the yard when it began, and soon a crowd of men were brandishing their arms . . . in my face, shouting and yelling with a noise and fury not to be imagined by anyone who has not seen an excited Chinese mob. They yelled into my ears and struck my chair with their tools to attract my attention, but I continued to sit facing them, never moving a muscle, as I was quite innocent of the cause of the quarrel, and at last they subsided and let me depart.' No pretence now that an English lady can travel anywhere in safety! But nothing turned her back until she met a solid wall of Chinese bureaucracy between herself and the further confines of the mountainous Mantze country which smelt of Tibet and where the 'jovial, laughing, frolicking people' drank chang. Travelling north up the Min river she struck west into the almost unknown valley of the Siao Ho, following it to its source in the Chiunghsia Shan, near Matang. Twenty-three years before she had stood with the 'frank and respectful' Comanche Bill on a high point of the Rockies where two great rivers of America flowed east and west to opposite seas; now in the hills which rise to the great plateau of Tibet she had found her way to an Asian watershed, at the headwaters of the Min and the Yalung. One's sympathies are rather with her companion Mr. Kay who, although 'strong and kind', was 'very absent', and must have been hard put to it to keep pace with this inexhaustible valetudinarian. She wanted, like all good travellers do, to cross the frontier—in this case from China into Tibet—and the more obstacles the local authorities put in her way the more determined she was to go on:

The scanty hoar frost lay on the ground at 5 the next morning, and the sun rose, as he had set, in glory, flooding the canyons with a deluge of amber light. There was a considerable delay before starting, and to the last I feared the wiles of Chinese officialism: but it turned out to be only the usual difficulty of the first start with animals—weighing and adjusting loads and the like. There were three strong, whole-backed, pleasant-faced red mules, and the muleteer was equally pleasant, a Mantze lama, quite a young man, who proffered hospitality for the next few days among his friends, inns having ceased. The thought of 'poisoned feasts' never crossed my mind! . . . Climbing the Peh-teo-shan spur by a long series of rocky, broken zigzags, cut on its side through a hazel wood, and reaching an altitude of about 9,270 feet in advance of my men, I felt the joy of a 'born traveller' as I watched the mules with their picturesque Mantze muleteer, the eleven men no longer staggering under burdens, but jumping, laughing, and singing, some of them with leaves of an artemisia stuffed into their nostrils to prevent the bleeding from the nose which had troubled them since leaving Weichou, the two soldiers in their rags, and myself the worst ragamuffin of all. There were many such Elysian moments in this grand 'Beyond'.

The summit is thick with poles, some of them bearing flags inscribed in Tibetan characters in honour of the Spirit of the Pass, and there is a large cairn, to which my men added their quota of stones. Fifteen or sixteen hundred feet below, the river looks like a green silk cord interwoven with silver. There is a sharp bend and a widening, from which rise two conical peaks, forest-clothed and craggy. Lateral gorges run up from the river, walled in by high, frowning, forest-covered mountains, breaking into grey, bare peaks, and crags gleaming in the sunshine. To the north-west the canyon broadens. Mountains rise above mountains, forest-covered, except where their bare ribs and buttresses stand harshly out above the greenery, and above them great, sunlit, white clouds were massed, emphasizing the blue gloom of pines; and far higher, raised by an atmospheric effect to an altitude which no mountains of this earth attain to, in the full sunshine of a glorious day, were three illuminated snow-peaks, whose height from the green and silver river, judged by the eye alone, might have been 30,000 feet! They might have been 'the mountains of the land which is very far off', for the lighted clouds below separated them from all other earthly things, and their dazzling summits are unprofaned by the foot of man.

Somo, the nominal goal of her journey, south of Matang on the far side of the Chiunghsia Shan, was reached after strenuous travelling through the hills, and reluctantly she gave up the idea of fighting for permission to press westwards to the Tibetan border town of Darchendo (K'ang-ting today), the point at which Annie Taylor came out of Tibet after her attempt on Lhasa.

Isabella Bird Bishop, 1831–1904

In May 1896 Mrs. Bishop reached the Yangtze again at Chengtu and boarding a flat-bottomed boat, floated the 2,000 miles downstream to Shanghai. In March 1897 she was back in London. The final pages of Miss Stoddart's *Life of Isabella Bird*, written with deep devotion in the minor key, reveal a dumpy, indomitable figure, clad in neat black or in Chinese brocade, in a state of almost perpetual motion. She moved house constantly, each new home being furnished with enthusiasm and abandoned with extravagant regrets, but never really lived in. Her journeys, even in England, were fraught with drama—the worst storm in memory overtook her on her way to a missionary meeting at Macclesfield—out with a friend at Tobermory she fell over a cliff—she stunned herself by running into a wall of Fulham Palace when the guest of the Bishop—she crushed her thumb in the door of a railway carriage during one of her frequent lecture tours. In her seventieth year she ordered a tricycle because she needed more exercise, but before she could enjoy its use she was off to Morocco for 'a rest'. She landed on the shores of Africa after being swung over the ship's side in a coal basket, camped out in a wet field in a storm, was able to ride thirty miles a day without fatigue on a horse so big she could only mount him with a ladder. Well might the Sultan of Morocco hope that when his hair was as white as Mrs. Bishop's he might have her energy! 'So I am not quite shelved yet!' she wrote home with understandable complacency.

After a year or two in England, she declared her health was too delicate to endure 'even the quietest life in London' and was packing her trunks for China when she fell really ill. She died in Edinburgh a year later, on the move to the last, from nursing home to lodgings and back, a circle of devoted women and intellectual men constantly around her. Limbs, heart and lungs failed, but still her brain was clear and lively and her iron digestion stood by her: her friends, dismayed by the invalid's capricious appetite, found she could be tempted by such unlikely delicacies as a Scotch bun, a game pie, a stuffed leveret. On 7 October 1904 she died, as she had lived, in flight from life's humdrum routines, under a hired roof, with her luggage corded and labelled for a strange port on the other side of the world.

II

Marianne North
1830–1890

He hangs in shades the orange bright,
Like yellow lamps in a green night,
And doth in the pomegranate close
Jewels more rich than Ormuz shows.
The Bermudas, ANDREW MARVELL

'WE can all work hard at what we like best,' wrote Marianne North, and when one looks round the North Gallery at Kew, at tier upon tier of her vigorous flower paintings, their occasional heaviness relieved by vivid colour and satisfying design, it is her immense industry that first strikes one. Then, one is amazed by the high standard of her work, its very excellence inducing, in the mass, an almost monotonous effect. Quality and quantity, in fact, go hand in hand, the result of nearly twenty years of travelling and painting, in the course of Miss North's self-imposed task of recording the world's tropical flora.

It is not surprising that Marianne North found Mrs. Bishop unsympathetic, a valetudinarian and an exhibitionist. Their backgrounds and temperaments were very different, and although Miss North could, and often did, 'scream with delight' at a red-crested chameleon or a long-sought lily, she was wholly a stranger to the kind of enthusiasm which plunged Isabella Bishop into the total immersion of baptism at the hands of Dr. Spurgeon. She was, perhaps, the most normal of the lady travellers. An individual, certainly, with a sufficiently original ambition and achievement to her credit, but with the edges rubbed off by a cultured and yet conventional upbringing. As her favourite ancestor, the seventeenth-century lawyer and statesman Roger North, wrote of his brothers: 'It was

54

their good fortune to be surrounded with kindred of the greatest estimation and value, which are a sort of obligation to good behaviour.' For this Roger North, her 'fourth great-grandfather', a lover like herself of music and painting and of country pursuits, Marianne had an 'especial respect'. Quarrels in an earlier generation had broken up the old family place at Rougham in Norfolk where Roger had lived and written his famous family biography *The Lives of the Norths*, and Marianne's seafaring great-grandfather settled at Hastings; it was here she was born on 24 October 1830.

Her father was 'from first to last the one idol and friend of my life' and her earliest memories were of riding on his shoulder along Hastings beach, the friendly fisherfolk crying, 'Make way for Muster North and his little gal!' Frederick North had been a favourite pupil at Harrow of Dr. George Butler, whose daughter Louisa was Marianne's life-long friend. He was at different times Liberal M.P. for Hastings and enjoyed a wide acquaintance among the scientific, artistic and political personalities of the day, men like Sir Edward Sabine, President of the Royal Society from 1861 to 1871, the botanist George Bentham, Erskine May, famous as a constitutional lawyer, and Francis Galton, archetype of the Victorian amateur scientist—who married Louisa Butler. Though she had little formal education, taking her history from Shakespeare and Scott and her geography from Robinson Crusoe, Marianne learnt young to be at ease in such company, although her own talents were artistic rather than scientific. But then, like all Victorians who cared for the things of the mind, Marianne was uninhibited by that tedious modern invention, the two cultures. Sir Joseph Hooker, Director of Kew, encouraged her, naming no less than five botanical varieties in her honour; Charles Darwin sought her acquaintance, and welcomed her in his domestic seclusion at Down. Travel was a formative influence. The family year was divided between Hastings in the winter and London in the spring, with a leisurely progress to Norfolk in the early summer, when Mr. North himself drove the family out of London through the sweet-scented lanes to Rougham. There were regular visits to Gawthorpe Hall in Lancashire, the property of Marianne's half-sister Janet, who later married the educationalist Kay Shuttleworth. To this sister, as well as to her own brother and sister, and to both her parents, Marianne was tenderly devoted and her happy, carefree childhood gave her, no doubt, that normality which is such an agreeable feature of her personality. At Rougham, where her brother's descendants live today, and at Gawthorpe, she is remembered as the beloved 'Aunt Pop' and her sketch-books and diaries are treasured.

Europe's 'Year of Revolutions', 1848, saw the Norths abroad for a spell; enjoying the charm of Heidelberg and alarmed by the siege of Vienna, they yet found time and opportunity for exploration of the countryside and, as far as Marianne was concerned, for strenuous and continual music lessons. It was at this time of her life she cultivated her fine contralto voice, and sometimes practised on her piano for eight hours a day. Mrs. North's death in 1855 brought Marianne and her father even closer together, and with him she roamed Europe, and went as far afield as Turkey, Syria and Egypt. In her early *Recollections* a forgotten world unfolds, an eighteenth-century world of diligences and couriers, of the heyday of the sketch-book, of bandits and picturesque peasants, and of Protestant prejudice which saw a Grand Mass at St. Peter's simply as an occasion when 'the poor old Pope tried in vain to get a pinch of snuff . . . he never to the end succeeded though he was infallible'. Betweenwhiles, Parliamentary sessions kept them busy in London, and their garden and the entertainment of their friends employed the time merrily at Hastings. Here an Italian cook, brought home from their travels, superintended the housekeeping, while in the London flat a truculent, but devoted, Norfolk woman provided a daily dinner of 'a nice shoulder of mutton'.

When Mr. North died in 1869 Marianne lost the one strong emotional attachment of her life. She fled abroad with Elizabeth, her faithful but exasperating lady's maid, in whose company she decided once and for all that 'the perpetual companionship of any one is to me very wearisome, especially when they have no absorbing object and work to do, when talk or perpetual motion are their only amusements'. Henceforth the London flat in Victoria Street was her home, becoming ever more crammed with objects brought back from her frequent travels—birds in glass cases and once-brilliant butterflies, disintegrating under the London dirt, a stuffed koala bear, platypus and albatross, weird musical instruments, collections of shells and, presiding over all with well-bred Victorian calm, a bust of her mother, in which friends saw year by year a stronger resemblance to Marianne. (Isabella Bishop's home in Edinburgh struck a more exclusively Oriental note, crowded out as it was with 'Eastern cabinets and the palms which stood in the *daimio*'s bath'.) Marianne's sister Catherine, who married the literary critic John Addington Symonds, writes of the 'warm, delightful welcome' her sister gave to everyone, and of how they all wished Aunt Pop would stay at home for ever, to love and be loved by her adoring family. But she was a dedicated traveller; she 'had long had the dream of going to some tropical country to paint its peculiar vegetation in natural abundant luxuriance', a dream which began to take shape, perhaps, when she painted her first landscape one summer with her beloved father in the Pyrenees, and which, now he no longer needed her, she was free to pursue.

In 1871 she embarked on her first long journey, by way of Canada and the United States to Jamaica and Brazil. There was no tropical vegetation in North America, but Canada offered Niagara Falls, and Washington a visit to the White House 'I had a card brought me the next morning,' she recollected,

> The Secretary of State and Mr. Fish followed it, to whom I had a letter of introduction. He was a great massive man, with a hard, sensible head. He said he would call for me in the evening, and take me to the White House. So at 8 o'clock he came again after another big card, I being all ready for him in bonnet and shawl, and in no small trepidation at having to talk tête-à-tête with the Prime Minister in a small brougham. However, I found there was no need, as he did it all himself. We were shown in first to the awful crimson satin room which Mrs. G. had described to me, with a huge picture of the Grant family standing side by side for their portraits. Then we were told to come upstairs, and passed from state-rooms to ordinary everyday life up a back staircase, which was the only means of reaching the upper storey allowed by the architect of seventy years ago. We were shown into a comfortable library and living-room, where a very old man sat reading the newspaper, Mrs. Grant's papa, who did not understand or hear any of the remarks Mr. Fish or I made to him.

Then came Mrs. Grant, a motherly, kind body; then at last came the President, also a most homely kind of man.

We at first sat rather wide apart, and I had more of the talk to do than I enjoyed, and felt like a criminal being examined till Mrs. Grant hunted up a German book full of dried grasses to show me, and the poor withered sticks and straws brought dear Nature back again. I put on my spectacles and knelt down at Mrs. Grant's knee to look at them. They began to find out I was not a fine-lady worshipper of Worth, and we all got chatty and happy. Mrs. Grant confessed she had no idea 'Governor Fish had brought me with him, or she would not have let me upstairs, but didn't mind now'; and she told me all about her children; and if I had stayed long enough would, I have no doubt, have confided to me her difficulties about servants also. The two big men talked softly in a corner as if I were not there, and I watched till Mr. Fish looked like going away, and then I rose. They were all so sorry I could not stay the winter there, and hoped I would come again, etc. etc., like ordinary mortals; and Mr. Fish showed me a water-colour drawing of the Grants' country house, took me into a blue satin room, which he said was very handsome and conducted me home again . . .

The next morning I found a big envelope with a huge G. on it, and a card inside from the President and Mrs. Grant asking me to dinner that night. The G.s had another, so we went in state and were shown into the blue satin oval room, well adapted for that sort of ceremony, and the aide-de-camp General Porter came and made himself most agreeable to us. Then came two Senators and the Secretary of Foreign Affairs, and then the President and his wife arm in arm, with Miss Nelly and a small brother, and grandpapa toddling in after. He had an armchair given to him, and General Grant told me he was so heavy that he had broken half the chairs in the house and they were very careful about giving him extra strong ones now. After a terrible five minutes, dinner was announced, and to my horror the President offered me his arm and walked me in first (greatness thrust upon me) . . . I could not think what I had done to deserve all this; but after I left it came out. Mrs. Grant talked of me as the daughter of Lord North, the ex-Prime Minister of England. I always knew I was old, but was not prepared for that amount of antiquity.

Marianne arrived in Jamaica for Christmas, and lost no time in setting up her easel, hiring for £4 a month a derelict house on the hillside outside Kingston, overgrown by the luxuriant vegetation she had come to find. Camping on the veranda, with a huge bunch of bananas hung like a chandelier from the roof, she settled down to paint, cared for by two old negro servants, and establishing thus early in her peregrinations her favourite routine of work:

> There was a small valley at the back of the house which was a marvel of loveliness, bananas, daturas, and great *Caladium esculentum* bordering the stream, with the *Ipomoena bona nox*, passion-flower, and *Tacsonia thunbergii* over all the trees, giant fern-frond as high as myself, and quantities of smaller ferns with young pink and copper-coloured leaves, as well as the gold and silver varieties. I painted all day, going out at daylight and not returning until noon after which I worked at flowers in the house, as we had heavy rain most afternoons at that season: before sunset it cleared again, and I used to walk up the hill and explore some new path, returning home in the dark.

Brazil came next, and here she struck lucky in making friends with the Gordon family with whom she stayed eight months at the gold mines at Morro Velho in the inland state of Minas Geraes. They understood her thoroughly, giving her warm hospitality and perfect freedom to botanize, to paint and to observe nature. When the hot weather came they took her to the hills and she spent a fortnight blissfully alone with the caretaker in a vast old ruin of a house in the heart of the virgin forest:

> I used generally to roam out before breakfast for an hour or two, when the ground was soaked with heavy dew, and the butterflies were still asleep beneath the sheltering leaves. The birds got up earlier, and the Alma de Gato used to follow me from bush to bush, apparently desirous of knowing what I was after, and as curious about my affairs as I was about his. He was a large brown bird like a cuckoo, with white tips to his long tail, and was said to see better by night than by day, when he became stupidly tame and sociable, and might even be caught with the hand. One morning I stopped to look at a black mass on the top of a stalk of brush-grass, and was very near touching it, when I discovered it to be a swarm of black wasps. When I moved a little way off I found through my glass they were all in motion and most busy. When I returned again close they became again immovable, like a bit of black coal, and I tried this several times with always the same effect; but foolishly wishing to prove they really were wasps, got my finger well stung. This little insect drama was in itself

worth some little discomfort to see. The brush-grass on which these wasps had settled was itself curious, each flower forming a perfect brush—a bunch of them made the broom of everyday use in the country; scrubbing-brushes were generally formed out of half the outer shell of a coconut.

One had always been told that flowers were rare in this forest scenery, but I had a great many, and some of them most contradictory ones. There was a coarse marigold-looking bloom with the sweetest scent of vanilla, and a large purple-bell bignonia creeper with the strongest smell of garlic. A lovely velvet-leaved ipomoea with large white blossom and dark eye, and a perfectly exquisite rose-coloured bignonia bush were very common. Large-leaved dracaenas were also in flower, mingled with feathery fern-trees. There were banks of solid greenery formed by creeping bamboos as smooth as if they had been shaved, with thunbergias and convolvulus and abutilon spangling them with colour. Over all the grand wreaths of Taquara bamboo, and festoons of lianes, with orchids and bromeliads, lichens and lycopodiums on every branch.

It was in Brazil she first met with hard travelling, in crowded coaches and trains and on the long ride from the railhead to Morro Velho on muleback, floundering through seas of mud and sometimes soaked to the skin with rain. A linsey petticoat, a woollen mackintosh and a large straw hat formed the basis of her wardrobe, a garb she varied little during the years, appearing at a smart concert in Viceregal company in India in 'my old serge gown and shabby hat'. Nothing incommoded her, except the cold weather which shrivelled her up, made her head and teeth ache and brought on 'a return of my old pain'.

The pattern of Marianne North's travels now becomes clear: the quick, warm friendship with the local settlers and officials, with or without the benefit of introductions from her influential circle at home; the kindly and considerate attitude to servants and natives, the attitude of a Victorian lady accustomed to good service and well knowing how to deserve it. Contacts made and attendants engaged, she spent only enough time with her hosts of the moment to satisfy her high standards of courtesy, before she took off into the forest or up the mountain. Established in happy independence, the days were not long enough to paint and paint and paint the glories of the tropical world she had come so far to find. For causes and questions she cared very little, her genius not being a political one (she could deplore the tiresome necessity her father was once laid under of having to fight a contested election). Marianne's preoccupations were personal and her approach to the world's problems empirical, its ills to be solved, where solution was possible, by private benevolence. Her views on slavery, encountered for the first time in Brazil illustrate this very well:

Almost all the menial work in Rio is done by slaves, either for their owners or for those their owners hire them out to serve; for though laws are passed for the future emancipation of these slaves, it will be a very gradual process, and full twenty years will elapse before it is entirely carried out. It would have been better perhaps if our former law-makers had not been in such a hurry, and so much led away by the absurd idea of 'a man and a brother'. I should like some of the good housewives at home who believe in this dogma to try the dear creatures as their only servants. One of my friends had been settled in Rio nine years with no maid-servant, only two black men (the lesser evil of the two), and some of her experiences were amusing. The blacks never kneel (except on the outside of illustrated tracts), and if they were told to scrub the floor they brought a pint pot full of water, which they poured over here and there, then put a bit of rag under their feet and pushed it about till the floor was dry again. If a black servant were spoken rudely to, or found fault with, he ran away back to the owner who let him out, and said he would not stay; his health would be ruined in that place, and his owner's property would be thereby injured in value. A good working man-slave could not be hired for less than £30 a year, though he might be fed and clothed (in slave fashion) for threepence a day: a girl for housework got £15 a year and two suits of clothes, besides sundry presents to herself to keep her in good humour, and prevent her from running away to her real owners. It is a mistake to suppose that slaves are not well treated; everywhere I have seen them petted as we pet animals, and they usually went about grinning and singing.

And from contemplation of these ungrateful blacks, Marianne turns with something like a relief that her readers share to an exquisite description of:

A large caterpillar, who built himself first a sort of crinoline of sticks and then covered it with a thick web; this dwelling he carried about with him as a snail does his shell, spinning an out-work of web round a twig of his pet tree, by which his house hung, leaving him free to put out three joints of his head and neck, and to eat up all the leaves and flowers within his reach; when the branches were bare he spun a bit more web up to a higher twig, bit through the old one, jerked his whole establishment upstairs, and then commenced eating again. He had a kind of elastic portico to his house which closed over his head at the slightest noise, his house shutting up close to it like a telescope; and then when all was quiet again out came his head, down dropped the building, and the gourmand again set himself to the task of continual eating. He ate on for some months incessantly, using his claws to push and pull dainty bits down to him, and shifting his moorings in a most marvellous way. At last the sleep of the chrysalis overtook him, and finally he became a very dowdy moth.

Passages like these, and they are frequent in Marianne's *Recollections*, demonstrate the influence of her father's scientific friends. Liberated by the theory of evolution from a static conception of the universe, the Victorian scientist could enjoy, in every fresh discovery about the natural world, a stimulating sensation of adventure, one might almost say of romance leaving him no time for speculation on the nature of God and the destiny of man. Over Marianne North, patiently absorbed in the tiny complexities of a caterpillar's cocoon, falls the benevolent shade of Charles Darwin, for whom no one of earth's creatures was too small to repay study.

Back in England for a spell in September 1873, she busied herself in various ways—taking lessons in how to etch on copper, and visiting Netley hospital where she helped to nurse her cousin Dudley North invalided home from the Ashanti wars. She also attended the British Association meeting at Belfast in August 1874, and later in the year took refuge from the cold winter of 1874–5 in Teneriffe. Here she again found a mountain retreat, reached on muleback, and settled in to paint at her ease on the same lines as in Jamaica. Her next long journey was when she joined some friends bound for Japan by way of America. Landing at Quebec in the summer of 1875, they made their way westwards by way of Salt Lake City, pausing to shake the hand of Brigham Young ('horrid old wretch!'). Marianne broke away on her own to visit one of California's great redwood forests and the Yosemite valley. She was the 'right sort' the local people decided, waving aside her tips, she 'cared for neither bears nor Ingens'. But though she fell in love with the great sequoias, wandering among them for hours, it was the wrong time of year to see the country at its best and she rejoined her friends at San Francisco. Japan was 'attractive', but though she accomplished much work, enjoying particularly the animated scenes in the towns and around the temples of those crowded islands, the cold was bitter and she arrived thankfully in the warm sunshine of Singapore in January 1876.

In Sarawak, staying with the 'White Rajah' Charles Brooke and his handsome, kindly wife, she recovered slowly from the rheumatism induced by the cold of Japan, and even had a new dress made from Chinese silk. It was while staying in Sarawak that she concluded that 'those long European dinners . . . are a mistake so near the Equator', and she escaped to the Rajah's mountain farm of Mattange:

> The Rajah lent me a cook, a soldier, and a boy, gave me a lot of bread, a coopful of chickens, and packed us all into a canoe, in which we pulled through small canals and forest nearly all day; then landed at a village, and walked up 700 feet of beautiful zigzag road, to the clearing in the forest where the farm and chalet were. The view was wonderful from it, with the great swamp stretched out beneath like a ruffled blue sea, the real sea with its islands beyond, and tall giant trees as foreground round the clearing, which was also full of stumps and fallen trees grown over with parasites—the most exquisite velvety and metallic leaves, creeping plants, 'foliage plants', caladiums, alpinias, and the lovely cissus discolor of all manner of colours, creeping over everything . . . Life was very delicious up there. I stayed till I had eaten all the chickens, and the last remains of my bread had turned blue; then . . . I came down again, my soldier using his fine long sword to decapitate the leeches which stuck to me by the way.

Another mountain excursion led her to the discovery of the largest of all pitcher plants, the *Nepenthes northiana*.

Java, where she went next, was 'one magnificent garden of luxuriance . . . with the grandest volcanoes', and 'under the strong rule of the Dutch the natives have a happy independent look one does not see in India'. As for the Botanic Gardens, always an early port of call for Marianne, enabling her to find her bearings among the local flora, it was 'a world of wonders'. She spent some months in Java, travelling in carts and on horseback, enjoying the colourful markets, learning Malay and climbing volcanoes, and reached Ceylon by way of Singapore towards the end of 1876. In Ceylon she stayed with Mrs. Cameron, whose photograph of her, in an unbecoming green cashmere shawl, Marianne thought absurdly fanciful, not knowing, perhaps, that to be photographed by Julia Cameron was to make artistic history. And of course she visited the famous Botanic Gardens at Kandy.

In the autumn of 1877 she was back in Ceylon after a quick dash home, on her way to a long tour of India which was to include the great temples of the south, the wonders of Rajputana and a protracted ramble in the foot-hills of the Himalaya; for this mountain excursion she travelled in a litter perched on the heads of its bearers. She 'found it best not to look too much over the side, but never met with any accident'. As usual, she carried letters of introduction to governors and rajahs, and was persuaded from time to time to travel as a lady should, with an ayah as a personal maid. Also as usual, she preferred being independent, herself scolding a group of frightened villagers into repairing a leaky boat when a flooded river interrupted her monsoon journey from Naini Tal south to Benares; living alone in a bungalow at Delhi under the shadow of the lofty Qutb Minar; and repeatedly dismissing those ayahs—'useless and without tact'. She much preferred the attendance of an old orderly who cleaned her shoes and brushed her clothes, and of 'my ugliest coolie, a giant with a most wicked expression' who 'crept into my room one afternoon and gave me a bunch of scarlet potentillas and buttercup flowers tied up with grass . . . Sometimes as we went on he would stoop down, pick up a few tiny flowers by their heads and fling them on my lap with a Caliban grin.'

She had so many paintings on her return to England that, in the summer of 1879, she hired a small London gallery to show them to her friends. Out of this grew the idea of a permanent home for them at Kew, to be built at her own expense. First, however, her collection must be complete and, regarding as a

Royal Command Charles Darwin's suggestion that she should visit Australia, she set sail in the spring of 1880 with Rajah and Mrs. Brooke, staying with them on her way to the Antipodes.

She enjoyed Australia, approaching from the north, visiting Thursday Island and coasting along the shores of the Cape York Peninsula. She landed at Brisbane and stayed at Government House, which opened conveniently on to the Botanic Gardens. She toured Queensland during the Australian winter of 1880, and was fascinated by the strange vegetation and stranger animals—the gum trees and eucalyptus, the koala bears, the parakeets and the platypus. Riding southwards by horse and coach into New South Wales, she rejoiced in a grove of 'magnificent old araucarias' and her first sight of kangaroos. It was said that she and her travelling acquaintance 'Miss B.' were the first ladies to travel that road alone by Cobbe and Co.'s coaches, and a double ration of beef was ordered in their honour at each wayside halt—likewise a double bedroom, at which Miss North strenuously protested. And she really preferred bread and butter to beef. After the long journey, partly through desert, came the sophistication of Melbourne, which offered concerts and a picture gallery; Western Australia introduced her to a fellow flower painter and traveller Ellis Rowan— disguised by Marianne in her usual unaccountable way as 'Mrs. R.'—and to the *hakea* 'like a tall hollyhock with leaves like scallop shells' and 'one of the most remarkable plants of the world'. The Governor telegraphed from Perth that she was to have the use of a carriage with a police driver as long as she wanted it, and she toured the south-west tip of Australia between Albany and Perth, the increasingly unreliable O'Leary on the box and the whole equipage mounted on an equally unreliable set of wheels. 'We passed only three houses in a sixty mile drive,' runs the account of one day's travelling:

And could get no food, but my Irish police driver boiled his 'billy' and made some tea at Black River, where the water was worthy of its name. However, we ate all we had with a better appetite than those who have abundance at home, and divided our few biscuits with Black Johnnie, the policeman's Man Friday, whose Irish was almost as incomprehensible as the language of the natives; but he was very kind to me, and managed to avoid the deep ruts, and to keep the old carriage very cleverly from accidents. It was a kind of 'inside car' with two seats sideways—one for myself, one for my portmanteau, and a bit of canvas spread overhead on four poles to keep the sun off. I had a tin biscuit-box half full of damp sand on the floor to put rare flowers in; but the sand soon ceased to be damp, many of the flowers drooped as soon as they were picked, and the whole carriage, as well as the box, became full of them. It was impossible not to try to keep the beautiful things for the chance of being able to paint them. At Rogenut I lodged at a police station, and was so surrounded by policemen calling me 'your ladyship' that I felt like the Queen of the Cannibal Islands, and rather a dangerous character. The sundew grew into perfect little trees near there, and we passed a mile of everlasting flowers, one perfect bed of them in the burnt-up grass. Then we came to another marvellous sandy plain, and every kind of small flower—great velvety 'kangaroo's feet', with green and yellow satin linings, exquisite blue or white lobelias, bordering the road like a hedge, and whipping one in the face as the carriage pushed through.

She finished her tour eating Christmas pudding with a family living thirty miles from the nearest town among groves of white gum trees, and after her rough travelling with O'Leary she was glad to return to the comforts of Melbourne and from there to go on to Tasmania. The island was a disappointment, chiefly remarkable for the purchase of three tiny marsupial mice who became her inseparable travelling companions. But it was cold and too like England to be interesting, and she set sail for New Zealand, cradling the little mice in her hands to keep them warm. New Zealand was cold too, bringing on rheumatism and a gumboil, and rather spoiling her visit to her cousin John Enys at Dunedin. He collected for her a sample of the curious 'vegetable sheep', a growth of tiny flowers on rock easily mistaken for a sheep lying on the mountainside, which she took home as a present for Charles Darwin, but even a delightful walk in Wellington Botanical Gardens and a sight of the perfectly formed cone of Mount Egmont did not reconcile her to New Zealand, and she and her mice were glad to reach the warmer air of Honolulu. Pausing only to admire the 'sensible bloomer costumes' in which the Hawaian ladies rode (Isabella Bird called them dainty) she took ship for America and from San Francisco made her way again to the redwood forests inland.

The North Gallery, Kew.

Marianne North as a young woman.
'I said simply I had done them all.'

Fanny Bullock Workman sight-seeing in Mysore and exploring
Siachen, the Rose Glacier.

'The New Woman was a late Victorian phenomenon.'

'We reached the redwood forests all of a sudden, and the railway followed the Russ river through them up to Guerneville, a pretty wooden village with a big saw mill, all among the trees, or rather the stumps of them, from which they have acquired the common name of Stumptown. The noble trees were fast disappearing. Some of the finest had been left standing, but they could not live solitary, and a little wind soon blew them down. They had a peculiar way of shooting up from the roots round the stumps, which soon became hidden by a dense mass of greenery, forming natural arbours; and many of the large old trees were found growing in circles which had begun that way: a habit peculiar to that tree.

The little inn was capital; and all the gentlemen of the place dined in their shirt-sleeves, and were much interested in my work. They told me how to find the biggest trees, but everyone was busy, and not a boy was willing to act as guide or to carry my easel. There was no difficulty in finding the trees; only in choosing which to paint, and how to get far enough away from such big objects as to see the whole of any one . . . there was an under-growth of laurel and oak, and many pretty flowers: pink sorrel, trillium, aquilegia, blue iris, and a deep pink rose. I got back to Oaklands after the supper hour (8 o'clock); but the porter brought me a large plate of crackers and butter, a tumblerful of the most adorable iced mixture, and a straw to suck it through.

In fact, Marianne's preference for bread and butter as a staple diet is worthy of mention, and could open the way to a disquisition on the eating habits of Victorian lady travellers. A return visit to the Yosemite valley introduced her to a charming fellow traveller, an old gentleman from Philadelphia whose 'energy and love of all that was grand in nature' recalled her father; it introduced her too to a squalid little camp of Indians on whom she made the rather unenlightened, and not un-typical, comment: 'Those who have sentimental ideas of the cruelty of the white races in driving out the blacks have not even seen the little I have seen of them or they would soon change their ideas.' She was to be impatient on her African journeys with 'Zulu lovers', and complacent, as we have seen, about the slaves in Brazil. The train journey across America was as physically restful as it was mentally exciting. She stopped off here and there, noticing, painting and recording; enjoying a noble garden at St. Louis, admiring the fine sweep of the Mississippi river, and exclaiming at the excellence of the Zoo and Palm House at Philadelphia, the mice as ready to make friends as was their mistress. 'Got into your right place at once?' asked the guard when she boarded the train and went straight to her bunk at Cincinatti. 'It's a way I have,' she replied, settling herself under the comfortable opossum rug. And presently she was in New York, treated like a lion and soon tired of 'perpetually roaring'.

In June 1882 the North Gallery was opened to the public. She had chosen a site 'far from the usual entrance gates as I thought a resting place and shelter from rain and sun were more needed there, by those who cared sufficiently for plants to have made their way through all the houses'. She would have liked refreshments to be available, but the idea of '77,000 people all at once possibly on a Bank Holiday' was too much for the Kew authorities to face. The building was designed by James Fergusson, the architectural historian, and expresses his ideas of how the Greeks lighted their temples. She asked Francis Galton, at that time Honorary Secretary to the Royal Geographical Society, to help her with a map, but his ideas were too elaborate to be practicable; the professional cartographer, Trelawney Sanders, whom she commissioned, did some 'exquisite hand-shading' but omitted to follow her instructions on the limits of palm and fir forests; so she paid for the work and abandoned the maps. She contented herself with arranging the pictures methodically by continents, labelling them meticulously, and providing a catalogue. The whole was set off by panels of rare woods; when finished, the gallery contained over 800 works, painted in oil on cardboard. Then as now, visitors were astonished by the number and variety of the pictures. 'One day, when the door was accidentally left open, some ladies and a gentleman came in. He was rather cross at not finding Sir Joseph, whom he was seeking. He turned rather rudely to me, after getting gradually interested in the paintings —"It isn't true what they say about all these being painted by one woman, is it?" I said simply that I had done them all; on which he seized me by both hands and said, "You! then it is lucky for you that you did not live 200 years ago, or you would have been burnt for a witch."'

In 1882 the collection still lacked an African section and Miss

North set sail for the Cape to repair the omission. Her journeys inland from Cape Town, and on the south-east coast between Port Elizabeth and Grahamstown, trekking by ox-wagon or by coach, followed her now familiar pattern. She stayed with bishops; she stayed in modest farmhouses and inns. As ever, the flowers, the birds and the beasts evoked her wonder and the people she met a kind of detached affection. True, she did not like the Boers, and the 'Zuluism' in Bishop Colenso's house (the walls hung with portraits of Cetewayo) distressed her, but between these extremes she was much at her ease. In the following year she visited the Seychelles where she painted some of her most attractive pictures and brought home a prize in the form of the hitherto unclassified capucin tree, *Northia seychellana*. 'Near the house were groups of huts, wedged between boulders, and thatched with the great fan leaves of the coco de mer,' she writes:

> The stalks forming ornamental points at the corners, and finishing the roof into a curve like the gates of a Japanese temple. There were many of these trees on the island of Curieuse, and a path was cut to one of the biggest, with a pile of boulders behind it, on which I climbed, and perched myself on the top; my friends building up a footstool for me from a lower rock just out of reach. I rested my painting-board on one of the great fan leaves, and drew the whole mass of fruit and buds in perfect security, though the slightest slip or cramp would have put an end both to the sketch and to me.

Agile and confident as ever, one would say, yet it was on this journey that her health began to give way. Becoming increasingly deaf, she was oppressed by noises in her head and by alarming nervous tension. She who had never feared to be alone with her flowers and her paints, barricaded herself into her hut in sudden, irrational fear of her life.

She recovered sufficiently to accomplish one final task: alone of the world's great trees the *Araucaria imbricans* or 'monkey puzzle' was not 'represented "*At Home*" in my gallery', and in November 1884 she left for Chile to seek it. Despite a return of her nervous trouble and a cold, stormy voyage through the Straits of Magellan, she attained her goal, climbing up into the mountains above Santiago, to be rewarded not only by her tree but by the glorious flowers of the 'great blue puya'. She died in 1890 after four years only in the house she had retired to at Alderley in Gloucestershire, where she had designed a garden stocked from all over the world.

To describe Marianne North's journeys in detail would take nearly as much space and time as she took herself in *Recollections of a happy life* and *Further recollections*, three volumes in all edited after her death by Mrs. Addington Symonds, from a much longer manuscript. The *Recollections* repeat the initial effect of the Gallery: there is a certain monotony, relieved, if one is patient by the moments when she 'screamed with delight', by spirited accounts of her adventures and misadventures, and by little anecdotes, told with a touch of good-natured malice, of rival travellers. Though telling us much of where she went and of how she got there, Miss North says very little about her methods of work. Her sister declared that she 'painted as a clever child would, everything she thought beautiful in nature, and had scarcely any artistic teaching'. Her real love had been music, but when, as a young woman, her voice failed her, she turned to painting. 'Intolerant of Rules' she evolved her own spontaneous attack on the beauties of the visible world, and her pictures are flowers-in-a-landscape, not flower studies for a lady's boudoir, or botanical diagrams. The coral palm of Brazil, whose brilliant tassels frame a perspective of sea and sky, was no single specimen, but one of the 'endless varieties of form and colour which make up the tropical forest' which was so different from the 'woolly looking woods of Europe'. The weird cacti of the Arizona desert were caught from the train as she travelled across America. The temples of Japan and a stretch of South African bush country alike provided conversation pieces of humans, birds and shrubs. She valued her pictures for their immediacy, painting fast and hard to catch the flying moment. Although exceptionally good-tempered and kind, she was maddened by the 'unthinking croquet-badminton young ladies in Darjeeling' who, when the heavens opened in a cascade of monsoon rain, asked why she had brought her sketch indoors to do? 'I take it out to be rained on,' she snapped, 'which makes the colours run faster, and that's the way I paint, as you say, so quickly.' She took all nature for her province—even man, when he added to the landscape by creating beauty, whether in a market full of life and colour, or in tree-shaded temples and imaginative gardens. Thus she could see, in the tapering column of the Qutb Minar, a likeness to the great Californian redwood which, with all the world's forests to choose from, was the tree she loved best.

PART THREE

The Champions

III

Fanny Bullock Workman
1859–1925

'Amen,' quo' Jobson, 'but where I mean to die
Is neither rule nor calliper to judge the matter by,
But Himalaya heavenward-heading, sheer and vast, sheer
and vast,
In a million summits bedding on the last world's past.'
Jobson's Amen, RUDYARD KIPLING

THE 'New Woman' was a late Victorian phenomenon, formidable, foolish or just funny, according to the temperament of the beholder. She wore sensible clothes and aspired to the professions, was broad-minded in matters of art and literature; she often smoked and nearly always bicycled; she always believed in women's suffrage. A writer in *The Queen* early in 1896 rejoiced that the New Woman had taken the place of the overworked Old Maid as a subject for jokes; another, later in the same year, saw signs of the Bachelor Girl becoming more talked of as a social wonder, and one might be sure that the 'clingy vine' type of female was 'as out of date as last year's sleeves'. Met in the pages of late Victorian and early Edwardian novelists, the New Woman seems to middle-aged readers today to resemble one of those masterful, elderly aunts who, in one's youth, made a refreshing change from the cosier and more conventional type. Actually, of course, the New Woman was far from elderly—she was young, avant-garde, even shocking, and it is surprising that more of our lady travellers do not fall into this category.

The type is represented, as far as one can equate any individual with any imagined type, by Fanny Bullock Workman who achieved more than passing fame as a Himalayan mountaineer and who, though married, was certainly no 'clingy vine'. The Workmans were Americans, rich and energetic, who visited the Karakoram eight times between 1898 and 1912, climbing, discovering and surveying, and scandalizing the Old Guard of British India by the vigour of their researches and the confidence of their claims. That Fanny was so evidently in the lead of all their enterprises offended the prejudices of what, in the golden afternoon of the Raj, was an exclusively man-dominated society. Fanny and William were forty and fifty-two respectively when they attacked the Himalaya first, and they arrived on the scene early in the hot weather of 1898, having bicycled from Cape Comorin to Peshawar—Fanny wearing a topi adorned with the badge of the Touring Club de France, and with a tin tea-kettle perched on her handlebars. She was born at Worcester, Massachusetts, on 8 January 1859, the daughter of a former Governor of the State, Alexander Hamilton Bullock. A conventional New England education was given a useful polish in Paris and Dresden, and in 1881 she married William Hunter Workman, a local doctor. Ill health is said to have forced his retirement, and in 1889 they went to Europe to find congenial 'opportunities for mental culture in music, decorative and dramatic art, and literature'. They lived for a while in Germany. Presumably the Doctor's health improved for, in 1890, when (as he put it himself) 'the bicycle began to come into fashion as a vehicle for women', they embarked on a series of cycling tours. For the next ten years they were almost continually awheel, not only in Europe but, in 1895, in Algeria. 'Bicycle maps did not exist' but the Workmans were undeterred, arming themselves with 'steel-cored whips' to beat off the dogs which had much annoyed Fanny by attacking her voluminous skirts when she was awheel in Italy, and revolvers to cow extortionate or even murderous natives.

Algerian memories is the first of the Workmans' travel books, characteristically full of guide-book information and of such glimpses of the obvious as 'the Arab quarter is extensive and teems with Arabs'. The author makes light of the dangers and discomforts of the route, and seems more irked by having brown boots cleaned with blacking than by being benighted in unknown country. 'A bright cold morning saw us in the saddle at 6.15' runs a typical entry, 'With the ruins of Thamugas or Timgad forty kilometres distant . . . Our hostess thought the expedience of using our rovers for this expedition doubtful, said the country was wild and hardly safe.' But 'the wheel enthusiast is an optimistic fellow'; the Workmans enjoyed 'the zest given to an unconventional meal in the open air by an appetite sharpened by a good morning's work', and they achieved an impressive itinerary over the Atlas Mountains and as far as the fringes of the Sahara.

Fanny was both observant and opinionated, and her comments were reinforced by her own photographs, for like many of the Victorian travellers she was a keen 'kodakist'. The delight of the early photographers in their magic instrument comes over amusingly in her account of a picturesque group of camels with their driver at Biskra: 'As soon as he came within proper range the Kodak was snapped. His presence in the resulting picture with one foot in the air, furnishes an example not only of an object in motion but of what might be termed a photograph of a mental state.' Practical and censorious as she was, Fanny was not immune from the incurably romantic view of the East induced in the Western world by the reading of certain classics and by the vicissitudes of a temperate climate at home. 'As on February 17 we were resting under the olives, on the grass sprinkled with violets, primroses and anemones, listening to the babbling brook at our feet, and watching the passing Arabs, some on foot, some on horseback, with their veiled women sitting behind, it is like a scene from the Arabian Nights, and an effort is required to recall the fact that, one week before, we were living under the leaden skies of Germany.' But she was also ready to notice the pernicious effects of absinthe on the local population and to applaud the conscription of natives who might thus be taught 'habits of order and obedience to authority'. The lot of women in Algeria, always one of Fanny's first subjects of enquiry in a new country, called forth something of a *mot*: 'A nation can be judged by the position of its women with the notable exception of Germany.'

Sketches awheel in fin de siècle Iberia records their Spanish trip of 1897, when the press pursued for interviews 'the Englishman Senor Workman and his sposa distinguida' on their 'bicicletas magnificas'—the mistake in nationality was gladly accepted by the sensible Workmans who appreciated the increase in their bills when they were identified as Americans. *Sketches awheel* is the most agreeable of the Workman's travel books. It suggests a pleasing affinity with the young couple of today, exploring the continent in their Mini-Minor, in search of Don Quixote and charmed by the gracious Spanish farewell of 'Go with God'. ' "Adios, vayan ustedes con Dios" . . . these words were destined to become a sort of "Leitmotif" to cheer many a long day's wandering, but whether used by a Catalonian, a Sevilian or drawled out in the rich guttural of the Castilian, with the peculiar prolonged sound of the *o*, they were never commonplace, but ever rang a sweet music in our ears. Spoken for the first time by the *guardia* they acted like a stimulant as we rode off on the deserted chaussée.' Like their counterparts today Fanny and William were cock-a-hoop at being made welcome at inns of their own finding off the beaten track, and could make a good story of having to doss down in a room usually occupied by a doctor and crammed with his evil-smelling stock of medicines. It must at any rate have been better than the Algerian hostelry where they had to sleep in the bar. It was not all plain sailing and 'Go with God', however. There were 'rude mechanics' on the coast road to Barcelona which made it 'not pleasant for women' and further south, between Jijona and Alicante, they had dangerous altercations with teams of waggoners on the road. Knives were drawn but 'we had not come to Spain to measure our prowess with that of intoxicated teamsters; we never aspired to the glory of shooting them, nor did we court the notoriety of falling a sacrifice to their brutal passions.' Revolvers were put away, the Workmans rode on and beyond Murcia Fanny was able to report that 'we have taken grand rides, desolate rides and lovely rides, but never one so intoxicatingly beautiful as this through African Spain'.

Pleasant as it is to read of these early continental travellers, these pioneers on the Costa Brava, there is a certain insensibility which jars on one, allowing them to attend a number of bull-fights ('tauromachic revels') while condemning the cruelty to the bull and the brutalizing effect on the bull-fighter. And where was Fanny's New England conscience when, on an excursion to Tangier, she admired the 'bright, pretty slaves . . . in white and pink muslins' who served their coffee? And where her concern for women's rights when she observed without comment that their Arab host was a 'connoisseur who buys only the best'? Perhaps she did not expect much from Africa. Back in Spain, she was again on the qui-vive on her favourite subject and was disgusted, though hardly surprised, to learn from a fellow guest at an inn that Spanish women were excessively priest-ridden. An oddity characterizes *Sketches awheel* which appears in all their books, an evidently set policy not to mention themselves by name. Absurdity is reached in the description of a visit to a church in which women were required to cover their heads, so a mantilla was borrowed and 'one of us enveloped in its folds'.

In 1897 Fanny Bullock Workman and William Hunter Workman (as they invariably styled themselves) sailed for the Far East where they toured Ceylon, and 1898 saw their arrival at Cape Comorin all set to bicycle the length of the Indian subcontinent. *Through town and jungle: 14,000 miles awheel among the temples and peoples of the Indian plain* is a remarkable book as much for what it includes as for what it leaves out. Determined to inspect and record every temple and town, every mosque and monument on the route, they were singularly unmoved by the splendours and miseries of India—her captivating glamour and appalling poverty; the smell of evening fires; the timeless procession to the well; the village elders under the pipal tree; the sudden barbarities of her ancient religions; the infinite grace of her people—Fanny and William do not mention these at all. Not for them the romance of the Grand Trunk Road— Kipling's 'broad, smiling river of life' where Kim strode out the miles with the Lama—to Fanny its width was inadequate and its scenery dull. It is now one begins to realize that the Workmans did not really care for humanity.

Their longest run was eighty-six miles in one day. They forded rivers. They pushed their loaded bicycles through sand, ten or twelve pounds of luggage on the handlebars, including Fanny's kettle. They recorded sun temperatures of 160°F, and they once mended forty punctures in a day. They slept either in *dhak* bungalows, the staging posts of the old India, or in railway waiting-rooms. In the former, a caretaker might or might not be in a position to provide food; in the latter, one would be lucky to find a 'cane couch', but more probably they would have to 'sit the night out on uncomfortable straight backed chairs', a 'method of repose which did not serve to relieve fatigue any too well after a hard day's ride nor to fortify for the next day's equally severe exertion.' Their 'olfactory organs' were often assailed and drinking water was a continual problem. Their lot was sometimes alleviated, sometimes worsened, by the servant who travelled ahead to reconnoitre and prepare the night's lodging, and who was sometimes drunk and usually incapable by the time they arrived. When the roads became impossible they took to the train, but never did they fail to photograph, to record and to evaluate the stupendous architecture of India. To be emotionally moved by such wonders as the painting and sculpture of Ajanta and Ellora was not in their natures, but it is to Fanny's credit that she preferred the haunted red city of Fateh-pur-Sikri to the chill perfection of the Taj Mahal. With such travelling laurels, then, did the Workmans arrive in Kashmir and, by way of a hot weather relaxation, organized their first mountain excursion, which took them from Srinagar eastwards into Ladakh and as far as the Karakoram Pass, in the summer of 1898. An attempt to lead an expedition through Sikkim and on to the slopes of Kangchenjunga was made in September, but was abandoned owing to trouble with the porters. The advent of the cold weather saw them again awheel on an east-west traverse of India, and they followed this up by a tour of Java. Henceforth the 'trusty rovers' were put away and the Workmans became Himalayan explorers.

They were early in the field of that kind of serious sport which culminated in the 1953 ascent of Everest, an activity in which private ventures were to supplement the hard-won knowledge of the Survey of India. There had, in fact, been European travellers in the Himalaya since the early seventeenth century, but systematic and recorded discovery began with the British and is linked with the spread of conquest and influence into the vast ranges which outline India's frontier in an arc from Peshawar in the north-west to Darjeeling in the north-east. Penetration of the Himalaya was an important gambit in the 'Great Game' which Major Sawyer was playing when Isabella Bird Bishop travelled with him in south-west Persia, the object there as here being to checkmate Russia.

Fanny Bullock Workman, 1859–1925

The great age of discovery and survey begins, one may say, with the appointment of George Everest as Superintendent of the Great Trigonometrical Survey of India in 1823. The regular survey of Kashmir, where the Karakoram range lies, was initiated in 1846 and there were famous mountaineers there long before the Workmans made it their stamping ground —Montgomerie and Godwin Austen, Younghusband and Conway, to name but a few. But Fanny and William made their contribution. Their expeditions were well organized and staffed by experienced Alpine guides, and on several occasions by professional map-makers; they were infinitely courageous and persistent; they took really valuable photographs. On the other hand, they lacked sympathy with the local people and so had endless trouble with their porters ('coolies' in that unenlightened age), and they paid scant attention to the work of their predecessors. They 'discovered' regions already noted by earlier travellers, or sometimes undiscovered them, alleging that this or that peak did not exist, that Martin Conway, perhaps, or that famous Himalayan pioneer Tom Longstaff, had miscalculated a height, misnamed a pass or mistaken a cloud for a rock wall. Controversy hummed, enlivening the meetings of the Royal Geographical Society to which the Workmans regularly reported their findings. A lesser woman than Fanny, precluded at this date from membership, would have left her husband to do the talking, but this would not have been at all in character. It was she who addressed the Society in November 1905 on the 'First exploration of the Hoh Lumba and Sosbon Glaciers', when the usual contentious atmosphere surrounding the Workmans was masked, at any rate in the pages of *Geographical Journal*, by the old-world courtesy of the President, Sir George Goldie, in his introduction of the speaker. Skating over the undoubtedly still sore point of the admission of lady Fellows, Goldie pointed to the 'fine example' set by the R.G.S. to other learned societies by the award of the Patron's Medal to Mrs. Somerville in 1869. It was something of a triumph for Fanny to be invited to speak; she was the only woman to do so since Isabella Bird Bishop had addressed the Society in May 1897 about her journey in Szechwan. That Fanny was, or became, an experienced speaker is shown by her absence from William's lecture to the Society on the Nun Kun massif two

81

years later, when she was, explained the Chairman, 'engaged in something almost more arduous than climbing 23,000 feet. She is delivering thirty lectures in thirty-seven days, starting from Munich and going by Vienna up to Dresden, Berlin, Hamburg.' Legend has it that even when William occupied the platform Fanny supplied much of the material and she certainly wrote most of the books.

The Workmans came to the Himalaya from an exhaustive study of the temples and palaces of the East, in India, Ceylon, Java, Sumatra, Indo-China and Burma, and after so much of man's handiwork, cluttered as it was by shiftless, unreliable and disagreeably poverty-stricken humanity, Nature's handiwork made an immediate and lasting impression. From now on, the eternal snows were to govern Fanny's life, and therefore William's too. The vein of poetry which lurks in the most prosaic sprang to life and is rather finely expressed in the dedication to her first book, *In the ice world of the Himalaya*:

> He who has wandered under the shadow of the banyan, *pepul* and tamarind of India, the palms of Ceylon, the weird creepy trees of Siam, and the kingly *waringen* of Java, and has lingered by their stone duplicates and the *naga* forms, deftly cut upon the walls of the temples, can understand something of the motives of the bygone adherents of the Tree and Serpent worship, which led them to adopt these emblems of protection and power as objects of their adoration; emblems, which, after the disappearance of the original cult, intertwined themselves so persistently with both the Brahmanic and Buddhist traditions.
>
> So he, who has spent months among the silent glaciers and peaks of the icy wilderness on the northern boundary of India, can understand why the Men of the Hills should invest these temples, built by architects no man can emulate, with a sacred character, people their icy *cellas* with imaginary deities, and wreath their spires with the incense of a primitive folk lore.
>
> In sympathy with the sentiment, which inspired these early races and led them to appreciate the power and majesty of nature, we dedicate this narrative to the Abode of Snow, the thousand pillared ice halls, the grandly chiselled *gopuras*, the golden pinnacled *sikras*, that for fourteen hundred miles on the north form a dazzling chain of glory, protection and power to India.

Returning from their cycling tour in Java in June 1899, Fanny and William arrived in Srinagar, capital of Kashmir,

May French Sheldon takes the lead in Africa.

Fanny Bullock Workman displays a placard in the Karakoram.

'This outburst of female energy is undoubtedly linked with the increasingly vigorous movement for women's emancipation.'

Fanny Bullock Workman and her 'trusty rover'.

May French Sheldon afloat on Lake Chala.
'The exigencies of travel forced them into many odd conveyances.'

with a view to serious climbing with the experienced Swiss guide Mattia Zurbriggen who had climbed in the Karakoram with Martin Conway. Gazing out from their first camp across the Vale of Kashmir, that obstinate romantic streak in Fanny's character distracted her from the misdeeds of the porters and led her to notice that:

> Besides the beauty of Nanga Parbat, what chiefly attracts attention is the odd Kashmir-shawl appearance of the valley below. We mean the rare old pattern of the shawls possessed by our grandmothers which, like the antique vase of Japan and the embroidery of India, has vanished, except in collections like those that drape the walls of Raja Sir Amar Singh's reception room, or lie stored in the iron boxes of the Treasury at Srinagar. Nature in a mood of fantasy has preserved in the much praised 'Vale of Kashmir', this souvenir of the palmy days of Shah Jehan, more unique than the famed gardens of that Emperor, and nearly as valuable to the antiquarian as the beautiful temples of Martand and Payech. One has only to ascend a few thousand feet as to the Rajdiangan or the summit of Mahadeo, to see the bed of the valley transformed into a sheeny silken shawl of line upon line of green rice fields, and miles of sinuous waters ending in lotus-covered lakelets, or circling about brown sands bare of vegetation. One should not view it with the eye of the modern artist, but rather with the Oriental imagination of the aforetime Kashmiri designer, when it will show forth the ancient model ever renewed by nature at the melting of each winter's snow. The more one studies India, the more one sees, that its people copied nature in modelling their own handiwork; and this is as clearly the case with the temple builders as with the designers of the Kashmir shawl.

This second expedition included several impressive ascents of peaks which they measured themselves by means of aneroids, and named. Many of Fanny's heights were disputed, the more vigorously for being on the optimistic side and geared to insistently claimed records, and few of their names survive. The 'Siegfried Horn', calculated at 18,600 ft., 'Mt. Bullock Workman' at 19,450 ft. and 'Koser Gunge' at 21,000 ft.—this was the bag for 1899. Now that passions have somewhat cooled, it is surely possible to admire a middle-aged couple who could attain summits of this order (even give or take 100 feet), not once but over and over again in the years that were to come. On the debit side of this otherwise satisfactory trip, trouble broke out constantly among the coolies, 'stupid fellows' who 'chattered and gesticulated', showing an unaccountable distaste for high altitudes and rough going on to which they were led, or rather driven, without warning or explanation. Almost alone of Victorian travellers, the Workmans had absolutely no sympathy or even common-sense understanding of the local people, into whose poor and remote villages they burst with trains of followers demanding service and supplies. They had no plan for controlling the necessary labour beyond high wages: 'Contract, high wages, food, tents, tea, and tobacco, all of which were theirs in this case, make no impression, and after a few days' snow camping they cease to be the debonair, helpful individuals often depicted by the Anglo-Indian valley pounder.' Those who suggested the 'efficacy of kind treatment' (which meant 'coddling') were talking sentimental nonsense. Every now and then they employed a man with a glowing testimonial from some old hand, and sure enough he would give more trouble than anyone else. Fanny and William took great pains with their preparations, appointing each other leader of each expedition in turn, and allotting responsibilities to each other with scrupulous fairness, but they never learnt the knack of handling native labour. In their later expeditions, they partially solved the problem by importing Italian porters for the high altitude work. A clue to their local unpopularity may perhaps be found in a passage by Dr. Workman in which he complains of the 'unnecessary annoyance' of being importuned for medicine by the 'lame, halt and blind, malformed children, adults afflicted with incurable, organic diseases, and the aged staggering under the burden of senile, degenerative processes, a procession that would tax in vain the physical and intellectual resources of a thoroughly up-to-date hospital and staff of trained specialists'. It certainly taxed the resources of Isabella among the Bakhtiari, but she did her best and learnt from her ministrations more of the country she was travelling in than the Workmans, with all their zeal and efficiency, ever contrived to do. Dr. Workman complains, with quite unconscious irony, that such scenes recalled those 'depicted in Holy Writ'. It is typical of them, in a small way, that they should mention pigsties in the village of Arandu on the Chogo Lungma glacier, and show no surprise at pigs being kept in a Moslem village. Mary

Fanny Bullock Workman, 1859–1925

Kingsley would have wanted to know why they were there, and one wonders if, incurious of customs other than their own, the Workmans simply made a mistake, describing as 'pigsties' sheds which they were not interested enough to investigate.

In addition to their record ascents on this expedition, one rather spectacular descent occurred, of Fanny into a crevasse:

> From Ogre Camp the ascent is gradual but constant. We reached the entrance of Snow Lake, which lies at about 16,000 feet, at 2 o'clock p.m. The snow was now become soft, a good deal of water lay under it, and the crevasses, which were mostly covered by fresh snow, became more frequent. Here we roped as it was necessary to move with caution. The lightly-loaded coolies followed in our *spoor*. It is needless to say, that, with the wet snow and water under it, our pedal extremities did not suffer from dryness.
>
> The fatigue occasioned by a march can seldom be estimated by the number of hours required to accomplish it, and, certainly, that afternoon on Snow Lake may be counted as one of the most fatiguing afternoons on the Biafo. With all due care, we were constantly in snow or crevasses, to above the knees, and one of the party will not soon forget the sensation she felt on disappearing up to her shoulders in one of the latter.
>
> Zurbriggen said, 'Pull on the rope and push back with the feet.' This is good advice, when there is anything to push against, but pushing against space in a crevasse accomplishes little, and pulling on a rope, when one's arms are embedded in snow, is about equally futile, but finally, by strenuous efforts on her part and hauling on that of the guide, she came out again. This form of exercise continued until half-past four, when we began the ascent of an ice slant, where each step had to be cut. This took some time at a height of over 16,000 feet after the tumbling gymnastics of the afternoon.

And, as a grand finale to the trip:

> A strong gust of wind blew off the *Memsahib*'s treasured Ellwood *topie*, although fastened with elastic, and down it bounded with lightning speed over the slant of the great arete, across lower snow-fields, where it disappeared from view towards a huge crevasse nearly 1,000 feet below. It bore on its front a specially made Touring Club de France badge, that had travelled in many lands of Europe, Africa, and Asia, but was doomed to succumb to the elements on Koser Gunge. Let not sympathetic women think

85

the *Memsahib* stood bareheaded in the storm, for, fortunately, under the *topie* was worn a face mask, and cap with ear flaps. But it had broken the force of wind and sleet, which afterwards pricked, like a thousand needles, her partially exposed forehead.

In 1902 and 1903 they explored the twenty-eight-mile long Chogo Lungma glacier in the Lesser Karakoram, at the bifurcation of the Rakaposhi and Haramosh ranges. Measuring and surveying, they corrected the Survey of India and made some disparaging remarks about the veteran Godwin Austen, on whose swift plane-table survey of 1861 the official map was based. Time has had its revenge. When Wilhelm Kick, the German geodesist and climber, made his detailed survey of Chogo Lungma in 1954, he restored the map to its pre-Workman state, and put into perspective one of the Workman records. Confusing the peak now known as Malubiting (24,470 ft.) with one to the north-east (which Kick calls Yengutz Har and marks as 23,056 ft.), they claimed to have reached 23,394 on the latter, which they called Pyramid. The usual row with the porters broke out but when 'the ringleader made a fervid appeal to the Memsahib, begging her to return, he had no suspicion that she was the most obdurate person in the party, so far as returning was concerned'. Had Fanny by a miracle survived to the present day, Herr Kick would have had a task to prove to her that she had been wrong about Pyramid.

In 1906 their circuit of the Nun Kun massif, midway between Srinagar and Leh, took them less far afield but was the occasion for claiming another record—23,350 feet to the summit of Pinnacle Peak, and an altitude record for a woman. As with all too many of Fanny's triumphs, this effort, no mean one in itself, has been put in its place. Pinnacle, which the Workmans asserted to be the highest peak in the Nun Kun group, is in fact the third highest after Nun (23,410) and Kun (23,250); its established height is 22,810 feet. It is interesting to recall that Nun was ascended for the first time by the famous mountaineer the late Madame Claude Kogan in 1953, and that the massif did eventually prove the scene of a female record. It is to be hoped that Fanny would have rejoiced at this and at Madame Kogan's later achievement of 25,300 on Cho Oyu, but she would certainly have disputed vigorously the record claimed by the eight Chinese women who ascended Mustagh Ata (Survey of India height, 24,388 ft.) in 1959. She had a good deal to say about the American climber Miss Annie Peck who gave out that she had reached the summit of Huascaran in Peru, to which she gave, by any standards, an absurdly exaggerated height. Fanny sent a party to Peru at her own expense to measure the offending peak which came out, after all, lower than her own altitudes in the Himalaya.

In 1908 the Workmans explored the Hispar glacier of which they had had glimpses on earlier expeditions, travelling this time from Gilgit through the domain of the Mir of Nagar, examining the Biafo-Hispar watershed and returning on their 1898 route across 'Snow Lake'—the scene of Fanny's fall into the crevasse. The years 1911 and 1912 saw their most successful efforts when they explored the Siachen, or Rose Glacier in the eastern Karakoram. During the summer of 1911 they reconnoitred the west and south approaches to Siachen, and crossed the Bilafond La, or Saltoro Pass, into the valley of the glacier itself. To return in the following year and explore thoroughly one of the longest and most inaccessible glaciers outside the Polar regions was too tempting to resist, and they set themselves to a difficult problem of logistics. The tongue of Siachen ends not in a convenient moraine supporting a village, like Arandu at the tongue of the Chogo Lungma, where a base camp may be pitched, but in the turbulent waters of the Nubra river. Base would have to be at Goma some twenty-five miles away to the west of two stretches of glacier with the difficult Bilafond La, over 18,000 feet, between them.

This was an ambitious project for a private explorer without Government assistance, as one was faced with the undeniable fact that the Rose was not only the longest and widest in Asia, but incomparably more inaccessible from any proper base of supplies than any other great Karakoram glacier. Those who, like ourselves, have investigated glaciers such as the Hispar, Baltoro, and Chogo Lungma, all of which may be ascended from their tongues, will experience the shudder which the thought produces of visiting in its entirety a forty-six mile-long glacier with a useless tongue. I say useless tongue for the following reasons: the sparsely inhabited Nubra valley, devoid of large villages that can supply the needs of an explorer's caravan, winds its wild, uncultivated way north of Ladakh to the Rose glacier tongue. From this tongue issues the Nubra river, which in ever-increasing volume from the melting of glaciers above bears down upon the valley, cleaving it in the centre with its seething torrent. Some three or four fordings have to be made, from one side of the valley to the other, before the glacier-snout is reached, and these, between May and September 15th, because of the heights of the water and the numerous quicksands existing in the river-bottom, cannot be made by man or beast . . .

'No, I won't come again,' I said, as I sat snowed up in my tent for two days before returning over the Bilaphond La in September 1911. But no sooner had I turned my back to the Rose and reached again the top of the pass on that brilliant September 16th, than my mountain-ego asserted itself, saying *tant pis* to the obstacles, 'Return you must'.

Thus April 1912 again found us at Srinagar. Byramji was re-engaged as agent, and dispatched at once to Kapalu and Goma, where he was to take charge of collecting the large quantity of grain required to feed the caravan, of selecting coolies, buying sheep, and making general arrangements. Dr. Hunter Workman accompanied me, this time, in charge with me of commissariat and as photographer and glacialist, but I was the responsible leader of this expedition, and on my efforts, in a large measure, must depend the success or failure of it.

Kenneth Mason, in his classic work on Himalayan exploration *Abode of Snow*, shows himself no great admirer of the Workmans, but he concedes that their 1912 Siachen expedition was 'in a different category' from anything they had done before. Much was due to their securing the services of an outstandingly competent surveyor, Grant Peterkin, and to the loan by the Survey of India of one of their best men, Sarjan Singh, to plot the detail for Peterkin. The Survey and the Royal Geographical Society lent valuable instruments. The result is the highly professional map which accompanies *Two summers in the ice wilds of the eastern Karakoram* which, alone of the Work-man maps, has stood the test of time. The book contains also even more than the usual complement of those magnificent photographs which were Fanny's speciality. Among them is one of her standing on an eminence above the western source of the Siachen, which she called the Silver Throne, displaying a placard demanding 'Votes for Women'.

Fanny Bullock Workman, 1859–1925

It was a fitting climax to their travels. In 1914 war broke out, and in 1917 Fanny fell ill and, after eight years of suffering died, in 1925. William survived her by thirteen years living to the ripe old age of ninety-one. It comes as rather a surprise to the reader of their nine stout and rather indigestible books, lacking in any personal touch, to learn that they had a child—a daughter Rachel, who had an exemplary English education at Cheltenham and London University, graduating as a B.Sc. in geology. They called a mountain after her in the Chogo Lungma region in 1902. Rachel Workman won her own meed of fame, for she was the gallant Lady MacRobert whose three sons were killed in the Second World War, and who donated a Spitfire fighter to the Royal Air Force to be named 'MacRobert's Reply'.

The years have put Fanny Bullock Workman in her place. She was not a great Himalayan explorer; others had been there before and would go again to better effect. But she was a pioneer as none of the travelling sisterhood were—Marianne North, with her unique and unrepeated mission; Isabella Bird in search of personal and ever-elusive self-fulfilment; Kate Marsden obeying a call addressed to herself alone. Fanny showed the way, in her topi and veil, brandishing her irresistible ice-axe, to those women's parties and individual women who have climbed high in the snows, leaving in the magnificent collection of photographs which illustrate her books a legacy to climbers for all time. Above all, she loved the hills; perhaps that is her best epitaph.

IV

May French Sheldon
1848–1936

Where in jungles, near and far,
Man-devouring tigers are,
Lying close and giving ear
Lest the hunt be drawing near,
Or a comer-by be seen
Swinging in a palanquin.
Child's Garden of Verses, R. L. STEVENSON

'wow! Wow! Wow!' yelled the Masai warrior, hurling a spear which landed quivering at the intruder's feet; 'Wow! Wow! Wow!' carolled Mrs. French Sheldon, firing a couple of shots over his head, and briskly annexing the spear for the collection of curios which was one object of her safari to Kilimanjaro in the year 1891. Another, and equally important, object was to prove that where a man could go a woman could go too—and probably more successfully. Her African nickname of 'Bébé Bwana' attracts one to May French Sheldon from the start, and one is further charmed by the pennant inscribed *Noli me tangere* which fluttered from her alpenstock. To be sure, Bébé Bwana is merely the Swahili for 'Lady Boss', but it is not easy to rationalize that pennant. It reveals a delightful vein of feminine fancy in this brave, capable but rather humourless woman, endowing her with a charm notably lacking in her fellow American and contender for women's rights, Fanny Bullock Workman.

May was born in America in 1848. Her parents were well known in their day; Colonel Joseph French was a mathematician and May's mother is referred to in contemporary accounts as 'the celebrated Dr. Elizabeth J. French'. The place of May's

90

birth is not recorded, but though she had connections with Boston in later life the evidence points to the Frenches being a Southern family. Their considerable wealth was derived, partly at any rate, from plantations of cotton, sugar and tobacco and it is tempting to reconstruct May's background from her novel *Herbert Severance* which contains an undoubted self-portrait in Edith Longstreth who was born in Louisiana. Edith was taken by her parents to Europe when the American Civil War broke out and educated there. She grew up to be the close companion of her widowed father and of his men friends, developing a taste for sport and 'a broadness of mind thoroughly masculine'. Miss Longstreth, we are told, 'was a fine horsewoman, an excellent shot, and fenced well, could swim and skate, and manage a boat; in fact, loved all outdoor sports that gave her freedom to exercise muscles and limbs, and blow the cobwebs out of her brains'. We are assured, however, that 'she was not mannish, nor did she assume a certain horsy dash that some young women, who have cleared the first hurdle of small social orbits, are apt to adopt; adopt, too, in the mistaken notion that such assumption adds a certain air of independence to their personality, forgetting—if they ever knew—that strength of character can be as intensely feminine as masculine. No true woman seeks to enfranchise herself from womanliness.' All this accords so exactly with what we know of May French Sheldon that we hardly need to be assured that 'this young woman was utterly free from the mooted lackadaisical nature of a southerner'.

What is known for certain of May's family is that they were wealthy and cultured. Washington Irving was a close friend, and from the age of twelve May wrote stories and poems and amused herself with translations from French and Italian. She was largely educated in Italy, steeping herself in classical literature, in music and in art, returning to Rome after her schooldays were over to do research. She dabbled also in Mexican history, and in addition to a sophisticated acquaintance with the great cities of Europe she had something of a reputation as a big game hunter in the Rockies. At sixteen she made the first of four journeys round the world. Again one is thrown back on *Herbert Severance* in imagining that, like her hero, 'in true American fashion, I took the quickest steamship sailing for

Queenstown, *en route* for Paris via London; of course only tarrying in London long enough to hustle through and about the places of historical and local interest before I bolted off to Paris'. Here May's imagination takes wing, and Herbert goes on to describe the Bohemian life of the French capital in which he becomes enmeshed. 'I left Paris and its mocking whited sepulchres; the city in which I had for the first time pressed to my lips the dead-sea fruit of unmanliness; the city where I learned to trip the name of woman lightly, as though her spotlessness was of no more consequence that the beauty of the *boutonnière* that chanced to grace my lapel, but for a single evening.' Literary composition was not May's forte; the combination of Daisy Ashford and Ouida makes uneasy reading.

She grew up in a circle of her father's friends which included travellers and tycoons such as Henry Morton Stanley and his patron H. S. Wellcome. Stimulated, no doubt, by such company, she determined to travel in Africa, and studied geology and medicine—according to one account, she actually qualified as a doctor. She married, some time before 1886, Eli Lemon Sheldon, an American with business interests in London. They had no children, but Mrs. Sheldon found an outlet for her prodigious energy in literary work and in the management of her own publishing firm, Saxon and Co. of Bouverie Street, London, and of New York. In 1886 she published her translation of Flaubert's *Salammbo*. *Herbert Severance* appeared in 1889; naïve and melodramatic, it is nevertheless valuable in providing some clue not only to May's background but to her views. The most genuine passages in an otherwise absurd story are those in which Edith Longstreth states the feminist creed. 'Personal independence to a capable woman' she is made to declare, 'is a trait no sacrifice is too severe to make to secure. We seek work for another reason—we like to create something'. And she goes on with an honesty which makes one like her in spite of her extravant expressions: 'We often like the realization of personal power that the qualification to execute work brings.' Another side of May's character is reflected in her absorption in Flaubert's romantic and bloodthirsty tale. She worked on *Salammbo* for three years, turning it into blank verse and playing with the idea of dramatizing it. She dedicated the final prose translation to 'the man who created the Congo Free

May French Sheldon, 1848–1936

State, which is destined some day to outrival Ancient Phenicia' and 'whose exalted, noble attributes as man and friend excel, if possible, the greatness of his fame'. Stanley repaid this tribute by a review in *The Scotsman* in which he claimed that Mrs. French Sheldon's *Salammbo* 'made my blood course furiously through my veins'.

Early in 1891 May departed for the voyage which earned her a much prized Fellowship of the Royal Geographical Society. Her adventures are enshrined in *Sultan to Sultan*, a book which succeeds in maintaining throughout the resounding impact of its first chapter:

Ho for East Africa! possessed my brain when all the preparations possible to make before reaching Aden were completed, and a myriad of boxes and a bewilderment of nondescript packages— my tent, gun, table, chairs, pistols, photographic apparatus, and personal effects—had been sent by steamer to meet me at Naples, and for the first time I felt I was without doubt actually bound for East Africa. A hundred or more sympathetic friends and acquaintances, thronging the Charing Cross Station, albeit London was benighted in a pea-soup fog, thick, black, damp, and chilly, I was thrilled with ineffable delight. Gruesome remarks were intermingled with inspiring words of faith in my success: 'Well, you have my prayers for safe return.' '*If* you return alive, what a story you'll have to tell!' 'Do be reasonable and abandon this mad, useless scheme.' 'Brave woman, you'll accomplish all you aim to; we owe you a vote of thanks for your courage and self-sacrifice.' 'Be cautious, vigilant, ready for any surprise, careful of your health, and you'll win,' said Surgeon T. H. Parke. And A. Bruce, the sturdy son-in-law of the great Livingstone, thrust into my hands a long-range field glass, as if to bid me be far-sighted. 'Remember, nothing is accomplished without giving yourself up to the work at whatever sacrifice, and that honest failure is not defeat. We believe you will succeed.' His true words were branded on my brain indelibly, and echoed through my thoughts time out of number. Around me pressed lovely girl friends, sentimental hero-worshippers, who set the seal of admiration upon my lips by their farewell kiss, and whispered, '*How I wish I could go with you!*' Sedate man friends looked compassionately at my husband, and involuntarily calculated that the time would be brief ere he should regret his consent, which I had flouted widely, as evidence that when he sanctioned my undertaking, it was not irrational. We were off amidst cheers, pelting of flowers, and the usual half-hysterical, frantic commotion attending a departure when a friend's life seemed at stake. At last the cars were speeding away from London town, and my husband and two friends, H. S. Wellcome, Surgeon T. H. Parke, and myself were the sole occupants of the railway carriage, destined for Dover.

The journey to Naples was shadowed by anxiety for the traveller's Palanquin (always spelt with a capital P, it caused 'a veritable surprise' in Africa) which had cost eighteen guineas to register as personal luggage but was too large for the guard's van. At Naples she parted from Mr. Lemon Sheldon: 'the last ineffable look was interchanged, the handkerchief that had defiantly fluttered was soon saturated in tears,' and the sea voyage to Mombasa and Zanzibar was begun.

Bébé Bwana's goal was the dangerous Masai country north of Mount Kilimanjaro, first penetrated by missionaries from Mombasa in the 1840's, who astonished the armchair geographers with tales of snow mountains on the Equator. As Africa opened up to commerce and the 'Scramble' began, Great Britain and Germany both cast covetous eyes on the virgin tract between the stretch of coastland opposite Zanzibar and the Great Lakes far inland, while Arab traders ranged widely from their base at Taveta on the forested, south-eastern slopes of Kilimanjaro. The Masai, then a warlike people, were ticklish but potentially profitable customers. In 1882 Joseph Thomson needed all his skill and patience to pass through first Masai and then Kikuyu country on his notable journey from the coast to Lake Victoria by way of Mount Kilimanjaro and Mount Kenya. Stanley avoided the hazards of this route when he went in search of Emin Pasha in 1888, preferring to struggle through the Congo forests and to approach Lake Albert from the west. In 1885 the Berlin Conference recognized a British sphere of influence in Kenya, and a German one to the south in Tanganyika—both now independent African States. Great Britain and Germany had administrative posts along Bébé Bwana's route out from Mombasa and back to Pangani.

The practical aim of her journey was to study native customs and to collect examples of native handicrafts and weapons; equally important, however, was her desire to demonstrate that a woman could travel as easily and as effectively as a man,

May French Sheldon, 1848–1936

for May French Sheldon was a keen and combative feminist. Both aims received a discouraging check at Mombasa where she found awaiting her a letter from George Mackenzie of the Imperial British East African Company:

Despite the assurances I had had in London from important men in the directorship of the Imperial British East African Company that everything possible would be done for me, and even that they had taken the trouble to cable to their representative to use his best endeavour to procure porters for me, this gentleman evidently was neither interested in nor in sympathy with my 'novel enterprise', but, to the contrary, absolutely prejudiced against it. Like a flash I realized that without doubt he would, if he could, put a stop to the affair, believing, as he did, that my advent among the natives in the English occupation of East Africa would incur altogether too much risk upon the over-burdened company. Why, I could not imagine, as I did not ask, nor had I any intention of so doing, the company to act as my sponsor, or to contribute in any substantial way to my personal undertaking beyond giving me full permission to traverse their possessions, and possibly assist and advise me how to recruit a caravan. Henceforward I regarded Mr. G. S. Mackenzie as my *Obstacle*, silently bearing my chagrin, determined to quietly make my own arrangements, in so far as I could, without his knowledge or counsel, and when perfected, proceed with or without his permission, let the issue be what it might. Strange paradox, in the end matters culminated so that to this same *Obstacle* I owe a debt of gratitude. His maddening opposition developed and tried my metal, at the same time prepared me to encounter serious difficulties. I was convinced that it would be incompatible with prudence to attempt to start for the interior with a caravan until the rain came. Enforced patience held in check my impetuosity, awarding me ample time to perfect and mature my mode of procedure once I should start . . .

Alas! at Zanzibar I found that my world-renowned reputation of mad woman had preceded me, to my prejudice. In America, England, Aden, and Mombasa, and now here, I had to listen to and confront as best I could public censure. The bare idea that a woman should be foolhardy or ignorant enough to dare to enter Africa from the east coast and attempt to penetrate the interior as far as the Kilimanjaro district of the late Masai raids, at a time when great disturbances had been provoked by the Germans and a revolt was brewing, and essaying thus to do as the sole leader and commander of her own caravan,—the thing was pre-

95

posterous, and the woman boldly denounced as *mad, mad* principally because there was no precedent for such a venture; it was a
thorough innovation of accepted proprieties. It never had been
done, never even suggested, hence it must be impossible, or at
least utterly impracticable, and certainly outside a woman's
province . . . Having listened to these same sort of protests and
persuasions until my ears were dulled to their unsavoury
repetitions,—ay,e, in truth, I think I knew the formula of every
objection by rote and rule, and could ring the changes as deftly
as my opponents,—did these gentlemen know that my empire o
folly was not ostracized, and that I had received over two
thousand applications from both men and women, as a rule
accredited with unusual sense, occupying almost every rank in
life, and the majority of them professional and scientific men,
entreating me to allow them to accompany my free and independent expedition?

The determination of Mrs. Sheldon proved in the end too
much for the opposition and she enlisted the help she needed for
forming a caravan on the classic model, with a train of porters
to carry beads and cloth for barter and tribute, in addition to
camp equipment, arms, ammunition and personal luggage.
True to tradition, she packed an outfit in which to astonish the
tribal chiefs on ceremonial occasions—a court gown spangled
with artificial jewels and a blonde wig—the counterpart of the
full-dress Highland suit in which Sam Baker, discoverer of
Lake Albert, had done honour to Kamrasi, King of Bunyoro
thirty years before. Bébé Bwana recruited her porters in
Zanzibar, origin and centre of most important journeys into
East Africa in the latter half of the century. The Sultan's
authority extended to the coastlands and nominally for an
indefinite distance inland, and the American Consul arranged
an audience with His Highness for Mrs. French Sheldon. It was
galling for a 'free-born American woman' to be led through the
streets to the Palace as if for some quite different purpose, but
she put a good face on possible misunderstandings, and secured
such passes and permits from Seyyid Barghash as she needed.
There was a brisk trade going on in the interior at the time and
porters were at a premium but soon she had nearly 150 signed
on and, what was more important, reliable headmen and
interpreters.

In her pocket were directions for pitching camps from

May French Sheldon, 1848–1936

Captain W. E. Stairs, who had served under Stanley and had later annexed Katanga for King Leopold; in her medical chest were supplies recommended by Surgeon Parke, who had also travelled with Stanley; round her waist was strapped the 'M. French Sheldon medicine belt' with emergency remedies. Bébé Bwana 'looked with amazement over all these strange black and every shade of brown faces, with much brutality imprinted thereupon, and marvelled if I should always be able to control them and make them subservient to my commands . . . I felt somehow that I should'. She felt rightly: although Stanley was her hero, her methods resembled rather those of Joseph Thomson, the gentle and high-spirited Scot who receives in her book but one scant (and mis-spelt) mention. Like Joe, and unlike the dour, savage Stanley, Bébé Bwana enjoyed herself so much that the men enjoyed themselves too, and never has an African traveller had so little trouble with a caravan. Faced with a mutiny at an early stage, she drew her pistols from her belt, shot a vulture in flight 'to the astonishment of the revolting men', and compelled everyone at gun-point to take up their loads. Thereafter, though flogging was kept in reserve for the worst misdemeanours, the safari seems to have been a thoroughly happy one. Arduous tasks were offered as a challenge rather than imposed as a duty, and at the end of the day's march 'the dainty cloth was spread, the napkin placed, and the usual array of knives, forks, and spoons, and the enamelled dishes changed for each course', Bébé sitting down to dine in a silk gown. Porters wishing to air grievances brought a box for her to stand upon while she considered their case, she doled out the stores like a housewife and she used her guns like a man. For their part, the porters protected her from ants and avalanches as well as from thieving natives, and when she had a thorn in her foot the cleanest and most adroit of their numbers, after washing his mouth with eau-de-cologne, extracted it with his teeth. Like her contemporary Mary Kingsley, travelling at the same time in the French Congo, May French Sheldon was puzzled at being called 'Sir!', a form of address amended by Josefe the interpreter, who had been much at sea, to 'Aye, Aye, Sir!'.

The caravan was headed for Taveta, and on the way Bébé made friends with the natives, distributing rings with her name upon them and amusing them by such tricks as the making of a false set of teeth out of an orange skin. She was a zealous collector of objects and notions and her truly feminine interest in ornaments emboldened her personally to remove the leglets from the 'stark stiff body' of a Masai woman 'nosed out in the bush'. Her zeal for research sometimes led her to an odd conclusion, for instance that in tribes which have long practised circumcision this acquired characteristic may be inherited. An enquiry into the motive impelling primitive peoples to dance ended in the sage suggestion that 'it would seem to emanate from an indefinable species of voluptuousness'. 'Jambo! Jambo! Bébé mzunga?' (How do you do, lady white man?) cried the startled natives of old Kenya as she approached at the head of her train of porters, in neat walking dress and peaked cap, a crooked staff in her hand from which fluttered her *Noli me tangere* flag, the pistols they called her 'baby guns' at her waist, her dark spectacles thoughtfully removed for fear of alarming these children of nature.

From Taveta Bébé Bwana found a way into the crater, on the slopes of Kilimanjaro, where lies Lake Chala, and circumnavigated the lake in a copper pontoon left behind by Count Teleki, the Hungarian who discovered Lake Rudolf in the Rift Valley in 1888. On this feat subsists her claim to be considered a serious explorer:

> Standing on the crest of the rim of this crater, looking down upon the crystal water which was cupped therein, at first I was well impressed with the impossibility of descending to the water's edge unless some means could be devised as a substitute for flying. Nevertheless, on the assurance of Mr. A. of Taveta, who had some months previously descended to the lake edge, nothing daunted I determined to make the venture. There was a weird attractiveness overhanging this place that overawed even the natives. All accounts I could glean about it were so vague that I wanted to taste of the forbidden fruit myself. With an advance guard of only two men, alone, for Mr. A. remained at the top to direct the pontoon bearers, I found myself attempting to penetrate through a girdle of primeval forest trees, tossed, as it were, by some volcanic action against the rock base, and seemingly as impenetrable as any stockade. With bill-hooks and knives they cleared a slight opening through which I managed to squeeze, on emerging to find myself standing on a boulder, which was

Fanny Bullock Workman in a crevasse.

May French Sheldon in a palanquin.
'It is, of course, easy to be amusing about them.'

The Workmans in 1910.

'Fanny Bullock Workman (who took her husband along) and May French Sheldon (who left hers at Naples).'

Bébé Bwana pays
a state visit to a chief.

balanced upon another boulder, and every monent's tarriance seemed to imperil my equilibrium; and as I dared to venture on other uncertain surfaces which presented a footing, it required cat-like agility to crawl or slide down, sometimes landing in a bed of leaves, which must have been the accumulation of centuries, and into which I frequently sank up to my armpits, and had to be hauled out by main force by my men; and then by clinging and clutching to the branches of overhanging trees, after great effort and considerable peril, succeeded in laboriously attaining some other foothold, step by step advancing, again and again to be opposed by gigantic trunks of trees, which, lightning-smitten, had fallen as a barricade, or through some potent eruptive force had been uprooted and turned themselves top down in solemn humiliation . . . The weirdness of the scene was intensified by the strange whirring of birds frightened unceremoniously from their hitherto undesecrated homes, and the whisking of myriads of monkeys as they leaped from branch to branch without emitting a chatter in their fright. A whistling eagle beat the air with its wings directly over my head, scattering its feathers like storm-flawn flowers in its wild flight, and white-hooded owls peered out from sequestered nooks and twoo-hooed in solemn amazement . . . Through gaps in the massed trees, through which the sun could scarcely filter, the arboreal darkness was pierced by a radiant gleam of light, and the flashing lake greeted my expectant eyes. There arose a general shout from the men, 'Chala! Chala!' and behold! I found myself rewarded by being upon a rugged, rough tangle of prostrate trees and wild tumble of white and grey rocks, whilst the limpid, restless waters were laughing and dashing at my feet. The scene was one of which I became enamoured. It was truly overcast with a sublime sense of a holy sanctuary. Losing myself in the spectacle, I forgot that Mr. A. and porters, with the two sections of pontoons we had taken the precaution to bring, were waiting eagerly for me to give the signal agreed upon when once I should be safe at the bottom on the lake shore. After a moment's revery, recovering myself, I sounded the whistle. Then the deafening crash and yell and rush commenced, as the porters struggled valorously with their precious burden down the narrow, serpentine, rugged figment of a path, which we in the van had essayed to make . . .

So Mr. A., Josefe, and myself, with our guns and photographic instruments, embarked upon the bobbing pontoon with two long improvised paddles. We pushed carefully out from the shore, amid the shouts of the bewildered porters, who eagerly watched the performance, fully persuaded in their own minds that it must end disastrously, having taken the precaution to attach a hawser several hundred feet in length to the uncouth craft in case of accident. The crocodiles were very curious, not knowing what to make of the invasion of their haunt, and came in close proximity to our underpinnings, as with one paddle I manoeuvred to guide the craft and Josefe awkwardly propelled with the other, whilst my guest kept a sharp look-out for the obtrusive aquatic creatures. After moving the length of the hawser, we found the craft was manageable, and cut loose, to the horror of the men grouped on the rocks.

It was all very 'eldritch and immense' she concluded, with a typically bizarre choice of adjectives.

She made several descents to Lake Chala, flying the Stars and Stripes whenever she took the water in her pontoon, and when it was explored to her satisfaction she turned her attention to the local inhabitants, who had the reputation of being hostile. One cannot but smile at some of May Sheldon's more extravagant expressions and escapades, but she was no fool. She absolutely forbade her men to use their guns, even on wild animals, while she was feeling her way towards friendly relations with the natives. Then, suitably accompanied by four of her headmen and an interpreter, she paid a ceremonial visit to a village. She found:

> The delighted people most civil, and eager to do Bébé Bwana homage. They were neither uncouth nor unkind nor ungenerous, and certainly far from being hostile. They loaded me with gifts of beautiful furs and such other of their worldly possessions that I chanced to admire. Although, with few exceptions, men, women, and children were in an absolute state of nudity, the men carrying shields made of hippopotamus hide three feet long and a foot wide, bossed and with pressed designs, they brandished spears, the blade end not a foot long and narrow, carried bows and arrows, their deportment was as manly as one would naturally expect from civilized people. When they were presented by me with cloth (and this I wish to explain fully, because I have been very much misquoted on the subject), they looked about and saw in what manner my porters were bedecked. However, instead of putting their cloth on from a sense of prudery or shame, they were as likely to hang a piece of four or five yards trailing from their shoulder, or try to twist it about their heads as a turban, or tie it on to their arm or leg, as much so as they were disposed to use it

as loin-cloths or surround their bodies . . . They have no conscious-
ness of their nakedness. They bore themselves with so much
dignity, and I grew to regard their colour as abundant clothing
for them in their primitive simplicity. Truly they were clothed
with *toga virilis*, a robe of manhood unfashioned by any mode of
civilization, but inborn.

Mrs. Sheldon now set her caravan in motion again. and ra n
into the first serious opposition on her journey, in German-
controlled territory on the north-east side of Kilimanjaro. The
local chief hesitated to receive the white woman's emissaries, or
to give permission for her to pass through, but Bébé Bwana
merely marched straight on. She must have been feeling the
strain, all the same, to judge from the increasing number of
small accidents she met with. It is to this period, too, that
belongs the horrific episode described below:

One night, experiencing great fatigue, I fell in a profound
slumber lying in my Palanquin within my tent, when suddenly I
awoke with a shuddering apprehension of danger, and possessed
by an instinctive feeling of the presence of some harmful thing;
involuntarily seizing my knife and pistol I cried out, 'Who is
there?' No answer. Then I called out for the *askari* on guard, at
the same time tried to penetrate the darkness surrounding me,
when I became aware, through the atmospheric conditions, that
a cold, clammy, moving object was above me, in truth almost
touching me, on the top of my Palanquin, the rattans of which
were cracking as if under the pressure of a mangle. I was struggling
to slide out of the Palanquin without rising from my recumbent
position to avoid touching the thing, when the alarmed *askari*
entered, carrying a lantern, to my abject horror revealing to me
the object I had intuitively dreaded. My blood fairly seemed to
congeal in my veins at the spectacle: it was an enormous python,
about fifteen feet long, which had coiled around the top of the
Palanquin, and at that moment was ramping and thrusting its
head out, searching for some attainable projection around which
to coil its great, shiny, loathsome length of body. Seeing the
python, the *askari* immediately yelled wildly out for help, and in
a moment, a dozen stalwart porters pitched in a merciless way
upon the reptile, slashing and cutting its writhing body into inch
bits. I am not ashamed to confess it was the supreme fear of my
life, and almost paralyzed me. I came very near to collapsing
and relinquishing myself to the nervous shock; but there was not

time for such an indulgence of weakness; there were other sequences to be considered.

This was in 'primitive Kimangelia'; they now penetrated the borders of Masai-land, the secret goal of Bébé Bwana's journey. She had always found her chief headman, Hamidi, absolutely amenable to her orders, but when she disclosed her plans for a sally into the Masai country, he turned and said:

'Bébé Bwana, I will not conduct you thither; the danger is too great.' 'Then, Hamidi, do you mean to say that you disobey my orders?' He turned round and faced me, looking square into my eyes without hesitation, and replied, 'Bébé Bwana, I swore to the Sultan of Zanzibar and to Bwana Mackenzie to protect you as far as I could from all danger, and to give you my life rather than harm should come to you. Bébé Bwana, take these pistols,' and he drew his revolver from his belt; 'kill me, but I will not go.' There was a heroic majesty about the man; I took the proffered pistols, and whether he misinterpreted my movement I know not; he opened his *kansu* without demur, and stood stoically with his breast bared before me. 'I am ready, Bébé Bwana.' 'Hamidi, go, or I shall be tempted to do something rash. Let me think it over, and whether you go or not I go into Masai land. You and the rest of your goats may stay behind. I go into Masai land at sun-up tomorrow morning.'

Before daybreak I heard Hamidi's voice without my tent, saying pathetically, 'Bébé Bwana, I must speak to you.' 'Well, Hamidi, what is it?' 'I am sorry to have vexed you, Bébé Bwana; if you go into Masai land, I will go too. I might as well be killed one place as another.' And this fine man, as heroic and chivalrous and loyal as any white defender of a leader could possibly have been under the circumstances, succeeded in dissuading me from what would have been not only a most hazardous undertaking, but would doubtless have resulted in the entire looting of my caravan and annihilation of the Zanzibaris, no matter what might have happened to me.

She returned on a parallel route to the south, through the German sphere, visiting two powerful chieftains—Mireali of Marungu and Mandara of Moschi. Bébé allowed the latter ('waiving for once my rule of *noli me tangere*') to stroke her long golden hair; with Mireali she partook of 'a most notable afternoon tea', and promised to send him an umbrella and a saw. What should then have been a triumphal march back to the coast nearly became a funeral procession, when a bridge gave way, flinging Bébé in her Palanquin into the river. Shocked, bruised, suffering from dysentery and fever, she was carried to Zanzibar where she recovered sufficiently to pay off her caravan in person. 'A voyage of horrors' ended at Naples where her husband awaited her, the words 'Does she live?' trembling on his lips.

She did indeed, and by August was well enough to address the British Association at Cardiff on her daring exploration of Lake Chala. She could not, however, walk without a stick, and the audience noticed that she trembled either with weakness or because she was nervous. The President of Section E (Geography), E. G. Ravenstein, introduced her in warm and respectful terms, dwelling on her very proper insistence that her porters should be decently clothed; Sir Francis de Winton thanked her for her address, congratulated her on her achievement but did not advise other women to follow her example. In 1892 she was one of the select band chosen as the first woman Fellows of the Royal Geographical Society. Also in 1892 *Sultan to Sultan* was published, dedicated to Eli Lemon Sheldon 'to whom I owe all I have accomplished' and whose much lamented death occurred while the book was in preparation. In 1894 she was again on safari, this time in the Belgian Congo with the blessing of King Leopold, who gave orders that she should be afforded every facility for research among the natives 'throughout our Congo domain'. She certainly meant to write another book, but there is no trace of her having done so, and no account of her adventures beyond a rather obscure contemporary reference to having been provided with 2,000 coloured pictures, given to her by the journalist W. T. Stead and distributed along her route. On the outbreak of war in 1914 she went to America and worked hard raising funds for the Belgian Red Cross; for this, and for work in the Congo, she was made a Chévalier de l'Ordre de la Couronne by King Albert of the Belgians. She died in London in 1936, in a West Kensington flat, and her funeral was at Golder's Green—a prosaic end, perhaps, but Bébé Bwana had enjoyed so much of high adventure she could afford the dignity of a quiet passing.

PART FOUR

The Servers

V

Annie Taylor
1855–?

Farewell House! Farewell Home!
She's for the Moors and Martyrdom.
St. Theresa, RICHARD CRASHAW

'QUITE safe here with Jesus' wrote Annie Taylor in her diary
on Christmas Day 1892, crouched over a yak-dung fire in a fold
of the snowbound hills of Tibet. One is reminded of that other
missionary traveller, David Livingstone, assuring himself in a
moment of extreme peril that when Christ said 'Lo, I am with
you always', it was 'the word of a gentleman of the most strict
and sacred honour, and there's an end on't'. It is the authentic
voice of the Evangelical missionary, secure in a certainty of
personal salvation, for himself and for all mankind if they were
only given a chance to listen; convinced of an inescapable
summons to spread the Gospel. To such a missionary the Gospel
is quite simply the Good News, imperative to distribute,
impossible to withhold. To question the wisdom of changing
too suddenly a native religion and way of life, to await time and
place, to doubt the universal validity of the Christian message
is, to the missionary, sophistry and worse. This must be
realized before the modern reader can understand the tremendous drive which has sustained so many travellers in circumstances of extreme hardship, peril and disillusion. It must
certainly be understood in connection with Annie Taylor, who
was the first European to penetrate inner Tibet since the Abbé
Huc made his journey from the northern frontier to Lhasa in
1844–46. The Victorians were great missionaries. The Indus-
trial Revolution made them rich, the Evangelical movement,
which drew so much of its inspiration from Wesley and the

Methodist revival, gave them a conscience, and their immense vitality found a natural outlet in the slogan 'Commerce and Christianity'. Overseas markets opened the way to vast territories where the people sat either in pagan darkness or in what the missionaries regarded as equally deplorable—the thraldom of Islam, for example, or the negation of Buddhism. Of the activities of the Roman Catholic church throughout the centuries, the Victorian Protestants took little account, regarding as a virgin field such favourite areas as China. It was in the service of the China Inland Mission that Annie Taylor first came to know the Far East.

She was born at Egremont in Cheshire on 17 October 1855, the second child in a large and well-to-do family. Her father was a director of the Black Ball line of sailing vessels known in their heyday of a century ago as the 'greyhounds of the ocean'. John Taylor, a Fellow of the Royal Geographical Society, travelled much abroad, and somewhere in New Zealand a lake was called after him. Annie's mother had been born in Brazil where her father, Peter Foulkes, was a merchant. Mrs. Taylor could claim French descent not only from an aristocratic grandfather who had fled to Brazil to escape the Revolution, but from Huguenot forebears of the name of Gibaul. With these far-flung and romantic antecedents it is not surprising that the young Taylors grew up with a taste for far horizons.

Annie was a delicate child with a 'valvular disease of the heart', and not expected to live, a state of things which allowed her much of her own way and spared her the discipline of school. At some date in her childhood the family must have moved south for it was at Kingston-upon-Thames, when she was thirteen years old, that a conviction of salvation came upon her and she dedicated her life to religion. She had been a wilful, spoilt child; she became an enthusiastic Evangelical; in neither state was she easy to live with, being one of those people who never do things by halves. She gave up riding and dancing, she gave up the theatre; in and out of school, at home and abroad, dabbling in art, and all the time quarrelling (in the most high-minded way) with her parents, an uneasy adolescence passed until one day she was taken, during a brief period at school at Clarence House, Richmond, to a missionary meeting. The subject was the work of Dr. Moffat, the great pioneer of the Gospel in Bechuanaland, Livingstone's father-in-law, and the lecturer was Moffat's son. Annie determined to be a missionary and her resolution hardened through twelve years of argument with her father. She passed the time in visiting the sick in the slums of Brighton, where her parents lived for a time, and in London. This work, she maintained, was the basis of her later success in more dangerous venture. 'I found in the slums of London exactly as I have since in my Asiatic journeys, that a woman is rarely molested if she makes it quite clear that she is doing her duty quietly and unassumingly,' she told an interviewer from *The Queen* some years later, after her return from the East. She studied medicine both at the London Hospital and at Queen Charlotte's. When Mr. Taylor stopped her allowance she sold her jewellery and moved into lodgings. Family opposition crumbled at last, and on 24 September 1884 Annie sailed for Shanghai as a China Inland missionary. Mr. Taylor paid for her passage and her outfit, but he stopped her allowance again. He also guaranteed her passage home in the belief, or hope, that her enthusiasm would be short-lived.

Protestant missions had been active on the fringes of China since early in the century when Robert Morrison, the first Protestant scholar to attempt the translation of the Bible into Chinese, arrived in Canton in 1807. As the century went on increasing pressure on China by the trading interests of the Western powers had opened up areas of the interior hitherto forbidden to foreigners, and although the so-called Opium Wars of 1839–44 and 1856–60 were trade wars, the peace treaties which followed them gave increasing scope to missionaries as well as to merchants. Confined at first to Hong Kong and the Treaty Ports, by 1860 the adventurous missionary could begin to see his way inland. Such a pioneer was James Hudson Taylor who founded the China Inland Mission. He was the son of devout Methodist parents who had prayed that he might be a missionary in China, and as a young man he worked in the Treaty Port of Ningpo. His mind was haunted by the plight of the millions in China's interior who had never heard the Gospel, and he spent some years as an independent preacher travelling dangerously in areas not then open to the foreigner. In 1865 he and his wife, also a missionary, launched a campaign of prayer and exhortation for the founding of a mission

to the interior; by the time of his death in 1905 the China
Inland Mission had on its records over 800 missionaries
stationed throughout the Eighteen Provinces of China, and in
Mongolia and Manchuria. Taylor's system (for system it was)
was to pray for a definite number of workers to be called and
for the funds to meet their expenses, then to await God's reply.
In 1881 he prayed for seventy missionaries to come forward in
the next three years. In 1882 only eleven had been commissioned, funds were low and defections numerous. By the end of
1884, however, seventy-six missionaries had sailed for China,
the pick of the many who had applied, and money was flowing
in. The year 1884 was notable, too, for the enrolment of the
'Cambridge Seven', a group of brilliant and successful young
graduates which included the former stroke of the Cambridge
boat and captain of the Eleven. It was in this *annus mirabilis* that,
sped on her way by enthusiastic prayer meetings, Annie Taylor
sailed for China.

She was first posted to Chinkiang, the big Treaty Port near
the mouth of the Yangtze where she lodged in the Mission
House with Mr. and Mrs. Judd. As she mastered the language,
she joined in the fervent gatherings at the Mission at which the
singing of hymns and the expounding of the scriptures might
last from morning till night until the lady missionaries were
faint and hoarse; Mrs. Nicoll of Chungking once actually
collapsed with exhaustion and opened her eyes to find a group
of Chinese women fanning her back to life. Bible reading and
Sunday schools were regular features too, and all the time there
was a new way of life to learn—the Chinese way with a Christian purpose. 'Our sisters will become Chinawomen in dress,
custom, speech, and mode of living, in everything save in sin'
wrote a correspondent in *China's Millions*, the Mission magazine,
expressing somewhat naively Hudson Taylor's profound conviction that only by adopting Chinese dress and ways could a
worker make the close personal contact necessary to achieve
conversions.

At Chinkiang Annie began to absorb the peculiar flavour of
an enterprise whose watchword was *Jehovah Jireh*—'The Lord
will provide'—and whose scope was as wide as China's spiritual
needs. No salary was guaranteed, no collection taken or
personal appeals for funds made; the Lord did indeed provide,

and Hudson Taylor's organizing genius ensured that the provision was put to good and economic use. The Mission was broadly based, too, embracing all denominations, though doctrinally it held the strictest Evangelical views. And it worked. Whatever the number of volunteers prayed for, Taylor would accept no one for the Mission's service who did not come up to his own exacting standards of enthusiasm and efficiency. In the language of the revivalist, he asked that the men and women who came forward should be 'God-sent' as well as 'Godsends' to China. The Mission bred travellers, and indeed still does; one of the most notable explorers in the Gobi Desert in modern times was Miss Mildred Cable also of the China Inland Mission. The Mission's primary duty was held to be the influencing of as wide a circle as possible through preaching, through the distribution of tracts, and through continual personal contact. Once the ferment of the Gospel began truly to work in one place, messengers were to be ready with scrip and staff to move on to the next; the travelling preacher had priority over the static superintendent. One is reminded again of Livingstone, his imagination stirred by the 'smoke of a thousand villages' on the African horizon, where the Gospel was unknown. Women played a great part in the Mission's work and for some years before Annie's arrival had been travelling alone into the interior and even taking charge of stations. Not only was it an essential part of the Evangelical programme to set an example of Christian living, an example seen at its best in the life of the married missionary, but Hudson Taylor saw from the first what opportunities there were for the single woman who could move freely among her secluded Chinese sisters, urging them to study the Bible, to influence their menfolk, and to unbind their feet.

Such was the world of faith, hope and adventure into which Annie Taylor came at the age of twenty-eight. 'If we get the idea that people are going to be converted by some educational process, instead of by a regenerative recreation, it will be a profound mistake,' wrote Hudson Taylor whose personality inspired and informed every phase of the Mission's work. He called for 'workers not loiterers' and himself set a strenuous example in his personal determination to reach with the Gospel the furthest confines of China. He was constantly on the move:

on China's turbulent waterways sharing a cabin, perhaps, with a native convert; jogging over rough roads in springless carts; slung uncomfortably in a mule litter, or carried on the broad shoulders of a dedicated Cambridge rowing blue across a river in flood. So although little record survives of Annie's missionary service, it is easy to imagine her joining in the work of wayside preaching, calling the peasants, as they came at evening from the fields, to hear the Word of God, and spending the night in a village hut, perhaps sleeping in a straw-filled basket such as her contemporary Elizabeth Wilson describes. A new arrival, man or woman, might be lucky enough to travel with Hudson Taylor himself, learning in his company to sing hymns of thanks on the march and so earn the meal sure to be provided by the Lord round the next bend in the road, to travel by night when the day was too hot, and to tuck in the mosquito net before going to sleep, always to have a candle and matches for Bible reading in the early hours—a miscellany of knowledge which combined implicit trust in God with unremitting practical foresight.

Annie soon moved on to An-king upstream on the Yangtze from Chinkiang, a post which gave more opportunities of out-door work than the bustling, enclosed city, and in May 1885 she was writing that she and Miss Barclay were 'very happily settled with dear Miss Matthewson at the West Gate House. I do thank the Lord for bringing me out to China. He has indeed given me more than a hundredfold and I claim the promise made by God to Abram when he left his own country: "Thou shalt be a blessing." ' Late in the year she took 'two small journeys', one by boat; and a longer excursion preaching and teaching in the villages ended in a comfortable trip home 'in baskets'. The country people were much readier to listen than the more sophisticated townsfolk and Annie's aptitude for the work is shown by her posting in 1886 to Lanchow, capital of Kansu province in the north-west near the Tibetan border; here was crystallized the vague interest in Tibet which she had felt for many years. There was plenty to do: 'Lanchau is a very wicked city,' she wrote, 'The marriage tie is not looked on as sacred.' The women were exploited and despised: 'Who will come and raise them? They are going down, down into hell, and there is no one but me in this great city to witness for Jesus amongst them.' Yet she enjoyed being alone: 'God is so near. I feel more and more my nothingness and his omnipotence.' A Chinese Bible-woman joined her for a time and helped to teach such children as she could gather together. Mr. Parker, the scripture salesman, visited the city on his 700-mile round of Kansu, and no doubt sold in Lanchow some of the 3,000 portions of scripture in six languages (including Chinese, Arabic and Tibetan) disposed of during nearly three months of travel.

There was plenty to do in Lanchow, but just as Hudson Taylor as a young man had been oppressed by the darkness of inland China, so Annie now dreamed of the need of taking the Gospel into Tibet. Traders and pilgrims crossed the frontier fairly regularly, and once a year there was a big Tibetan gathering at Kumbum monastery near Sining, just east of the Koko Nor, the great 'Blue Sea'. Kumbum is one of the holy places of Tibetan Buddhism and the worshippers collected here offered a promising virgin field for the evangelist. Annie attended the annual Butter Fair and mixed with the crowd, distributing Tibetan text-cards and shaking her head over the jolly *chang* drinking parties. True to her single-minded purpose, she leaves no description of one of the strangest and least known sanctuaries of the world. The rambling lamaseries and demon-haunted shrines, the queues of shuffling pilgrims and the myriad priests in ceremonial yellow or red, which awed and bewildered as seasoned a traveller as Peter Fleming half a century later, stirred no romantic chord in Miss Taylor. Shining with votive butter the inscrutable images confronted the young Englishwoman with her testaments and her texts. She was not impressed; she invited the women to tea and her own home-made cakes, and in using her simple medical skill on their children felt she was coming a 'little nearer the hearts of the Tibetans and the lamas who were looking on'. But she could do little real good until she learnt the language, and when illness soon afterwards obliged her to return to Shanghai she took it as a sign that she must prepare for a new mission. Overturned by a drunken boatman on her way down the Hwang-Ho, she survived only to be told by the Shanghai doctors that she had consumption and must neither continue her work nor return to England. She recovered, however, completing the cure in the sunshine of Australia where her parents had cabled to her to join them. The hand of the Lord was shown further in an invitation from a married sister to visit her in Darjeeling. Here a cluster of missions would provide a background and a Tibetan community something to work on. Presumably the China Inland Mission approved, for her departure from Shanghai ' *en route* for Darjeeling to work among the Tibetans and study the language' is officially recorded in *China's Millions*, and her name remained on the books until 1893.

Towards the end of 1889 she arrived in Darjeeling and lived for five months at Ghum, afterwards crossing into Sikkim to be nearer still to her goal. The Tibetan frontier authorities regarded her with suspicion and she was moved on more than once, but her native obstinacy was unshaken. Living in sufferance in a corner of Tumlong monastery, she perfected her Tibetan and, by doctoring all who came to her, maintained a foothold in the hostile community. Thus she met Pontso, a Tibetan youth who had run away from his master in Lhasa, and under Annie's influence became a Christian. When one day in March 1891, she heard a voice say distinctly 'Go to China!' she left at once for Calcutta taking Pontso with her as her servant. She arrived at Shanghai determined to go to Tibet by the long route through China, and nothing her friends at the Mission could say would dissuade her from taking Pontso too. Very likely he risked being beheaded if he returned to his country, but it was part of her God-ordained plan to take him with her. It was really too late in the season to travel up country, but a freak flood swept her and Pontso in one boat (and, alas, a cargo of liquor in another) over the falling rapids, and three months later they settled down in the frontier town of Tau Chau to plan their journey.

In Tibet are clustered the most formidable mountains in the world and from their snowbound slopes and lakes spring many of the great rivers of Asia. There are no highways in Tibet, only ways, trodden for centuries by traders and herdsmen, by pilgrims and robbers alike. When the Abbé Huc made his famous crossing of Tibet he travelled with a regular caravan on one of the main routes, due south from the Chinese border, across the bleak, sour expanse of the Changthang to Lhasa. Fifty years later Annie Taylor and Pontso came in almost alone by a less

Kate Marsden en route for Siberia in 1890, and
presented at Court in 1906.

*'She desired passionately to help the unfortunate, she was very little concerned
with altering their condition in life.'*

Annie Taylor's Pontso and his wife Shigju.

Mary Kingsley's friends, the Fans.

'They were uniformly polite, considerate and condescending to servants and savages.'

well marked track, travelling west across the great loop of the Hwang-Ho, winding its way down from its headwaters in the lakes of Tsaring Nor and Oring Nor in the Bayan Chala Shan. Turning south near the lakes, and later west, they made their way to Jyekundo (which Annie called Kegu, the name of the monastery there) and then over hill and dale to Nagchu Dzong (Annie's Nagchuka). The route lay over cruel country, seamed and corrugated by the headwaters of the Hwang-Ho, the Yangtze, the Mckong and the Salween, flowing in a general direction of east and then south between the ranges over which, through the lofty passes, toil the yaks of the trade caravans. At Nagchu Dzong they were turned back, three days march from Lhasa. Retracing their steps to Jyekundo they left their old route for the quickest way out of Tibet to Ta-chien-lu, (now K'angting) sometimes called Darchendo, on the Chinese border. They took just over seven months on the journey and covered something like 1,300 miles.

The tracks of Tibet hold to the valleys, crossing where they must the rivers which rise and fall with the melting of the snows, climbing steeply to the barren passes, and falling again to narrow strips of farm land and pasture in the remote dales where the villages huddle in the shadow of the lamaseries. The people are hardy and high-spirited; xenophobic by instinct and tradition, they can yet be hospitable to the lone stranger and share with him their monotonous fare of *tsampa* and tea, varied by jugs of potent *chang*. Their women are picturesque, carrying their dowry in heavy jewelled headbands and crude ornaments; their children, strapped to their mother's back, are rotund and appealing. Of this wild and magnificent land and her noble people, Annie Taylor, preoccupied with the soul's salvation, contrives to give no picture at all. Like a good Victorian, she desires to instruct and from her stilted sentences and naïve drawings we gather certain facts—for instance, 'The Tibetans are a religious people . . . I was shocked to see men and women near Ta'ri'si, prostrating themselves the whole length of the road . . . Poor things, they know no better; no one has ever told them of Jesus . . .' The country, we learn from her conscientious jottings, is cold; there are many rivers to cross and mountains to ascend; the sun on the snow dazzles the eyes; deer and wolves, yaks and horses, eagles and ducks beset the paths. She shows no great interest in the natural scene; she does not observe the wild horses as Prejevalski would have done; she does not seek to divert her readers with the vagaries of the natives as did her near contemporary Thomas Thornville Cooper. Abbé Huc, whose literary style is more compelling and whose care for the soul was not (one assumes) any less must be consulted if we want to know what it was like to take a caravan across a Tibetan ford, men and animals crowding pell mell through the river and up the bank, the water freezing on them in icicles which 'jangled harmoniously', the whole presenting a 'hilarious' picture. More homely in her expressions, Annie merely thought that she and her companions looked 'fine frights' with their gowns tucked up to reveal bare legs and feet.

Miss Taylor's plan was simple: to travel across Tibet through Lhasa to Darjeeling, 'claiming the country for the Master'. True to her training, she made sensible, if modest, arrangements and left the rest to God—*Jehovah Jireh* and (the Mission's other watchword) *Ebenezer*, or 'Hitherto hath the Lord helped us.' She provided herself with two tents and food for two months; she had a camp bed and a box of 'presents for chiefs;' a few ounces of silver and some Chinese cotton represented her exchequer and she hired ten horses. She carried a pistol for defence and a telescope for observation. The elaborate canteens of silver, the tablecloths and titbits, considered essential by most Victorian travellers had no place in Annie's baggage. She packed two tin basins, a copper pan, a knife, fork and spoon and a couple of wooden bowls, and being rather an inspired cook managed to toss up some very tasty meals. She had in addition *Daily Light*, the New Testament and Psalms, an English hymn-book and a supply of Tibetan Gospels. Her one concession to convention was some English clothes to wear when she arrived in Darjeeling; for the journey she and Pontso dressed as Tibetans in wide-skirted, wide-sleeved, sheepskin robes. She hired three men to guide and carry: Noga, whose wife Erminie was a Lhasa woman, was an unlucky choice. Anxious to go with his wife to her home, Noga saw a chance of making some money by the way and agreed to conduct the party on terms which were never satisfactorily understood or accepted. As they got further and further from China, Noga became more and more afraid of the consequences of taking an Englishwoman into forbidden Tibet, he also became more rapacious and more unreliable until finally he was responsible for Annie and Pontso being turned back from their goal. Quarrels with Noga were a recurrent theme during the next few months, and when he was not arguing with Annie he was beating his wife, and sniping at Pontso of whom he became inordinately jealous. Leucotze was a Chinese Muslim, an absent-minded and rather lazy man, who succumbed to the intense cold and died on the way. Nobgey hardly developed as a character in the course of the narrative, because having failed to abduct a local belle to go with him (he told the unsophisticated Miss Taylor that she was his 'bride') he lost heart and turned back at an early stage. Penting, who joined the party at Kegu, was an amiable and faithful fellow, with very light fingers.

All this, however, was in the future when, on 2 September 1892, Annie and Pontso stole out of Tau Chau and slipped unnoticed over the frontier, joining the rest of the party and the main baggage in a dip in the hills. They went along easily enough in the first week, varying their basic ration of barley flour with mushrooms and a wayside gathering of raspberries, enjoying the mutton from a sheep purchased from a herdsman and making the surplus meat into sausages. Turned by a flooded river from the main path, they were soon in 'robber country' relying on local guides. Ambushed and plundered for the first of several times, Annie records that 'there were eight of them while on our side were only five fighting men', and she helped Erminie drive the baggage horses out of range. They found sanctuary in an encampment of black tents with a crowd of Mongol traders on their way back from Siberia, but even in company they were not safe. Hampered by the heavily laden yaks, they were set upon again, most of their goods were lost and their skins only saved in the general confusion. Nobgey had had enough, and decided to go home; here too began the disputes with Noga which were to bedevil the whole enterprise. Her neighbours in the camp took her part, and warned her against going on under Noga's dubious protection, but she refused to listen. 'The Lord is good', she confided to her diary, 'I will not fear what man shall do unto me.' By the end of September they reached the first arm of the Hwang-Ho and were floated over on bullock-skin rafts, and in the falling snow they trudged on through the land of the Goloks, or Ngologs, famous as bandits in a brigand infested land. They struggled through swamps and over hills to where the Hwang-Ho again barred their way. They fell in with a Chinese merchant who gave Annie a dress made of fox-skin, and for three days they waited for the river level to fall. 'The river is quite impassable, so they say,' she noted, 'but we are waiting until tomorrow to see if it will be lower in the morning. The Lord can do this for me. My eyes are unto Him who made a passage in the Red Sea for the children of Israel.' On 14 October they crossed under a snowy sky, the duck and teal flying south overhead. Leucotze, casual as ever, brought up the rear trailing a lead from which Annie's little dog had contrived to escape without his noticing. Camping exhausted on the far side, their rest was broken by Noga's constant quarrels with his wife; on the march again, Leucotze sickened and died, with the name of Allah on his lips—'The Master has called to account the strong, and left the weak to go on and claim Tibet in his name.' Wolves howled along their path and the men quarrelled among themselves, Noga increasingly jealous of Pontso, the lady's servant and cherished convert. By the side of the track, yaks' skulls lay white, a perch for the great black eagles swooping down vulture-like in the wake of the caravans. Travelling due south now in the full glare of the sun on the snow, Annie became weak and faint, sipping brandy and sal volatile while Pontso led the horse she was too feeble to guide.

From now on Annie's diary is full of river-crossings. They were travelling athwart the grain of the country, their way barred by the tributaries first of the upper Yangtze, later of the upper Mekong, and they are not always easy to identify from her diary. They came up with another encampment on the move and were carried with them across a ford in driving snow. 'Noga is frightened because they make remarks about my white face' she wrote, 'and want to know who I am. All must be right with the ambassador of the Lord. I am his charge.' On 31 October they crossed the Di Chu, or upper Yangtze, and after climbing 'the worst hill we have yet come to' took refuge in the house of a Tibetan couple, Penting and his wife. Penting agreed to come with them to Lhasa, and made such friends with Pontso that he persuaded him to worship in the local temple. 'The Lord forgive him!' wrote Annie, 'Poor weak Pontso! May strength be given him to stand.' November 10 saw them on their way again up the mountain, and so to the monastery of Kegu at the sizeable town and district head-quarters of Jyekundo, where they struck one of the main trade routes into Tibet from China, the 'Tea Road' from Ta-chien-lu to Lhasa. They began now to fall in with more traffic and there were trains of yaks on the road, laden with tea; a Chinese official alarmed them with questions. Annie's horse died under her and the tea which kept them going had to be made with melted ice and snow, the wind howled through them and Noga's demands and insults grew with his fears and jealousies. They camped with some merchants who were a protection from Noga's threats of violence and the leader of the caravan gave Annie a sound horse and provided some much-needed rations. She began to pray that Noga would leave them to find their own way to Lhasa. She had no more money or goods to placate him, and she really feared for her life. At last, with Penting and Pontso, she contrived to give him the slip and hide in a cave at Tashiling, reached after a week's travelling over the mountains. Here, though they had few belongings left, 'we have peace, and we are very thankful'. An important merchant, who was also a lama, now made his appearance and was very friendly, and with the arrival near their cave of a large and well-provisioned caravan on the way to Lhasa, they came in for feasts of mutton and red peppers, cheese and, luxury indeed, sugar. To crown all the sun shone with real warmth. Annie watched Noga and Erminie, who had caught up with them, ride away from Tashiling and felt at last she was quit of their menace. She sold her tent for eight rupees and set off again on her new horse, camping that night for the first time in the open. Free at last from quarrels and threats, Annie and her two faithfuls scrambled on up the hills and over and through the streams flowing south-east across their path to the parent Mekong. The crows swooped down to steal the meat off the ponies' backs, but there was enough for nightly suppers of fried mutton and barley flour. Once they lost the way, but she led them along the river bank, watering the horses where the wild deer came down to drink, and presently they found the track again. 'A nice Christmas Day' she wrote on 25 December, the sun shining brightly,' and she unpacked the suet and currants begged from the friendly traders at Tashiling and set about boiling a Christmas pudding. After two hours it was still not warm in the middle which, taken with the palpitations from which she had begun to suffer, indicate that their Christmas camp was high up in the mountains. She cut off her hair so as to pass for a Buddhist nun, and early in the New Year they came into Nagchuka (Nagchu Dzong on modern maps), the first place of any size they had reached since Jyekundo, where there was some sort of civil authority and where their business might be questioned.

Alas, Noga had carried out one threat at least, and had told everyone he met with that an Englishwoman was on the way, bound for Lhasa, and here it was that Annie reached the end of her road. She was hailed before a military chief, and remanded in custody, so to speak, until the arrival of the Governor. She was cool enough to notice that the chief was 'quite a dandy in his way, does his hair with a fringe in front and a fantastic plait at the back', and they were all quite polite to her, sending her a fore-quarter of mutton and some cheese. Interrogated by a subordinate magistrate she told him 'I must have courtesy, at which he seemed rather surprised. He said that I, being English, had no right to eat Tibetan food. I told him that I was a human being, not a wild beast, and that Tibetans coming to our country ate our food.' Told she must return by the road she had come, she retorted that this was quite impossible as she had no supplies, and that she had been robbed and cheated by Noga and his wife whom she demanded should be brought to justice. 'I had to be very firm, as our lives seemed to rest on my taking a firm stand.' The 'dandy chief' applauded her courage, and when an escort of thirty soldiers turned up to conduct her to the presence of a senior magistrate some miles away, 'I truly felt proud of my country when it took so many to keep one woman from running away!' While they waited for the arrival of the 'big chief' in whose hands Annie's destiny lay, they were entertained hospitably, Annie ordering her two men to light and boil her tea as usual because 'I have no intention of being a regular prisoner; so I act just as usual'. A statement was taken down in writing from her, in the course of which she was asked 'the name of my father and mother and my father's occupation.

As he is the head of his firm, I said he was a chief. My brother and brother-in-law both being in the Indian civil service, I was able to say that they were chiefs, too.' Pontso and Penting also made statements, describing Miss Taylor's kindness to them, and also her need of help and loyalty. Annie then set about washing 'my sleeves, so as to look a little respectable tomorrow when the big chief arrives', and watched with more interest than apprehension the pitching of the big black tent which was to serve as a court room. It was draped inside with curtains, and the chiefs sat cross-legged on high piles of cushions at one end, each with his own tea-table and steaming cup of tea. The back of the tent was crowded with soldiers and servants, the latter springing forward to fill the teapots from the kettle on the great brazier of coals.

Annie was not intimidated. She insisted on a proper mat to sit on; she refused to have Pontso or Penting bullied; but she knew she would not get to Lhasa this time, and that the lives of her two men were in even greater peril than her own. The stand she made in her clean sleeves was for good horses, sufficient provisions and a safe conduct over the quickest way out of Tibet for herself and her men; she also insisted that Noga, lurking in the background, should be forced to give up what he had stolen from her. Otherwise, she demanded that her case be laid before the Chinese *amban* in Lhasa—had the Acts of the Apostles been part of her daily ration of scripture? '*Ebenezer*' she must have whispered to herself as she knelt to pray each night, '*Jehovah Jireh*'. When she was threatened with being sent back to China with Noga on her own exhausted resources 'I said they might carry my corpse, but they would not take me against my will'. The night of 13 January was spent in prayer, and next morning first in comforting the tearful Pontso and then in attacking the magistrate. 'You want to send me on the road with horses which cannot go,' she stormed, 'And without a tent, knowing that in a few days we shall have to stop in a place where there is no chief, a place swarming with brigands; and thus seek to get rid of me, not killing me yourself, but getting me killed by others.' And she repeated her determination to stay where she was until her case was put to the authorities at Lhasa. Was this Tibetan justice, she asked, and she demanded the magistrate's name that she might report

him to 'the chief of our country'. The bluff came off; 'the chief
was much more civil after this,' and eventually she got most
of what she wanted—a horse, some of her goods reclaimed from
Noga, a sheep and some butter and, what was most useful, a
tent. The ten soldiers who were to escort her on her way were
led by the lama who had befriended her at Tashiling. On 18
January they turned back the way they had come, a big grey
wolf slinking across their path and the snow falling as they crossed
the first of the river branches between them and Jyekundo.

Half-way to Jyekundo their military escort turned back,
handing them over to a party of merchants, lumbering over
the hills at the pace of the slowest of their loaded yaks. It was
too slow for Annie and, dismissing the loudly voiced fears of
her companions, she insisted on pressing ahead. They had the
choice, she told Penting and Pontso, of freezing to death in
company, or of travelling light and fast and trusting in the Lord
to protect them from bandits. 'Very, very cold indeed' she noted
as they recrossed the passes, thankful for the tent which gave a
little shelter at night from the bitter wind. It was really due
to Penting that they got through at all. Twice he saved Annie's
life between Tashiling and Jyekundo, once when the ice gave
way beneath them on a river crossing and once when her horse
slipped on the brink of a precipice; it was Penting who killed
a hare they found crouching in the snow and cooked it for
supper (it made 'a nice change'); it was Penting who cheered
them by insisting that the wolves which crossed their path were
a good omen. The winter closed down relentlessly and the
drifts on the high ground became impassable, forcing them once
to make a circuit along a rock face and down a glacier, leading
the terrified horses. A caravan of merchants caught them up,
the last party to get through, they said, until the spring, and
now they were obliged to slacken speed and travel through
waist-high drifts in the tracks of the steadily moving yaks. Out
of the valley and over yet another pass, the two men walked to
save the horses, but soon first Penting's pony and then Pontso's
lay down to die in the snow. Pontso covered his with a felt
blanket and tramped away with tears in his eyes. They came
into Jyekundo on 21 February, the town *en fête* for the Chinese
New Year, and Penting found a comfortable lodging for Annie
with his sister. It is sad to relate that Penting himself, the gallant

knight of the road, lost no time in visiting the market where he was reported as getting a very good price for a number of articles which had been unaccountably missing from Annie's baggage for some time past; 'a hot water bottle sold for three rupees' she observed, with pardonable irritation, and she particularly lamented the loss of her English clothes. She was touched, nevertheless, when Penting came to say good-bye and wept to think of her going on alone with Pontso while he returned to his wife and family. He pressed his forehead to her's in the Tibetan fashion of farewell, and she gave him two horses, the tent, a sheepskin gown and ten rupees.

Traffic between Jyekundo and Ta-chien-lu, just over the Chinese frontier, was pretty regular but there were bandits about and Pontso was 'very frightened'. After a good deal of chaffering, in which Annie's watch changed hands several times, they made a fair bargain with a party going their way, and were glad to find a friendly young Chinese merchant in the company. They left on 7 March, riding through wooded hills and across a 'green, gleaming river', and on 18 March crossed 'the worst pass of the whole journey' when the sun was so bright they were in danger of sunstroke in spite of the bitter cold. They fell in with caravans, and came soon into cultivated country again where as many as fifteen yak-drawn ploughs could be seen in a field. The entry for 7 April runs simply: 'Gooseberry bushes! Wild apricots in blossom! The corn springing up in the fields! Green grass and—leeches!' On 13 April they arrived in warm spring weather at Ta-chien-lu where French Catholic missionaries took her in and were 'very kind'; two days later she and Pontso left for the coast. Five years afterwards the Rijnharts made their gallant and independent attempt to get into Tibet by the same road as Annie. Their child died on the way, and Peter Rijnhart never came back from the nomads' camp to which he went to ask the way. Susie Rijnhart's moving and graphic account of their tragic adventure gives one some idea of the danger Annie miraculously escaped. So also does the fate of the French explorer Dutreuil de Rhins who was murdered near Jyekundo in the summer of 1894 after a journey which must have covered some of the ground crossed by Annie in her traverse of the Upper Mekong tributaries.

Annie returned home to be lionized, and to fall into that familiar trap for the unsophisticated famous—she put her name to a book which gave a dramatic and by no means accurate account of her adventures, for which her admirers were still apologizing some years afterwards. She retained her self-possession, however, to judge from the interview she gave to *The Queen* in her lodgings in Earl's Court. The fragility of her build recalled Mrs. Bird Bishop, and the interviewer admired her hair, cut 'at the nape of the neck' to save her 'the impossible duty of hairdressing without conveying any suggestion of masculinity'. Pontso was with her, and seems to have been if anything a little above himself. Annie interpreted his remarks about the inferiority in beauty of Englishwomen to Tibetans; and no Tibetan woman would allow herself to be so hustled in the crowd as Pontso had seen happening to the English ladies when he went to the Mansion House to gaze at a Royal wedding. In Pontso's opinion, a mission from Tibet to England to teach the English courtesy was as much needed as any English mission could be in Tibet.

In addition to giving interviews, Annie lectured throughout England and Scotland, calling on Pontso to witness to the darkness in which his Tibetan brothers and sisters were condemned to dwell. She had set her heart on leading her own mission into Tibet and appealed for volunteers, in the manner of the China Inland Mission. The task of enrolling twelve missionaries and establishing a centre from so ill-provided a base as the hill country of Sikkim proved, however, to be beyond Annie's capacity. With a touch of arrogance she insisted on calling her group the 'Tibetan Pioneer Band', a name which even her friends and warmest admirers thought cast something of a slur on the labours of the French Catholics on the Chinese frontier in the north and of the Moravians in Western or 'Little' Tibet. On 16 February 1894 a prayer meeting was held at the Albert Hall to say farewell to Annie and Pontso, and five Scottish, one Swedish, two Norwegian and one English missionary. No women had been accepted for service, Miss Taylor deciding that the life was too hard for one of her own gentle sex, but one missionary brought his wife and little girl. After six months in Darjeeling, the Pioneer Band moved to Gnatong on the border of Sikkim and Tibet, a remote and dreary spot where lack of shelter and supplies tried the patience and enthusiasm of the party as severely as did the inevitable differences of opinion which arose between the group and its self-appointed leader. They broke up, the more enthusiastic joining Cecil Polhill-Turner's China Inland Mission station at Sining on the northern frontier.

Left alone, Annie settled herself into the best lodging she could find, a ramshackle hut on the mountainside below the old fort, which she shared with Pontso and his newly married wife Sigju. She named it 'Lhasa Villa' and from here she would walk out to visit the encampments of Tibetan traders, and join them at their evening fires, distributing texts and telling in her fluent Tibetan the Gospel story. From Gnatong she moved over the Jelep La to Yatung where, in May 1894, a mart was opened for the encouragement of trade between Tibet and India. Ever since the days of Warren Hastings, more than a century before, the British Government had been irked by the inaccessibility of Tibet, the unfriendliness of her rulers and the inscrutability of her Chinese overlords. To be able to enter Tibet for purposes of trade as freely as Tibetans were allowed to enter India, was all the British Government asked, and a series of tedious negotiations had, in the year after Annie's journey, culminated in the opening of the Yatung market. The British had wanted the mart at Phari, over the Tibetan border, but had had to be content with Yatung, situated in a narrow glen running into the main Chumbi valley, and enclosed by steep hills. Reporting six months after its opening, the Political Officer in Sikkim described the Tibetans as obstructive and discourteous, and complained that heavy dues were being charged on goods which crossed the Tibetan frontier. By the time the Younghusband Mission passed through in 1904, the Tibetans had built a wall across the valley to prevent free passage to and fro. With poky and inadequate shops and stores, rents five times what they were worth—sometimes as much as Rs.25 a month— Yatung could not have been commercially attractive, but it gave Annie promise of the access to Lhasa she longed for. She moved into her shop in 1895, sensibly deciding to be a trader in earnest and to stock cloth and calico, sweets and ornaments. William Carey, a missionary from India, visited her here in 1899; he found her a 'strange complexity of daring, devotion and diplomacy' and credits her with a sense of humour. We can believe she was a 'thorn in the side' of the officials at Yatung. William Carey and Annie talked for hours 'over the teacups in her little box of a room', and Carey handled with reverence the grubby little black notebook she took from a drawer when asked if she had kept a diary of her famous journey. This diary he afterwards incorporated in his own book *Travel and Adventure in Tibet*, doing posterity a service in putting on record the authentic account of Annie's lone and valiant attempt at storming Lhasa.

She was quite a local character by now, known to everyone as the Yatung *anni*, a Tibetan word meaning literally aunt, by derivation any respectable unmarried woman, by further derivation a nun—and a pleasing pun on her own name. Here her sister Susette Taylor visited her in 1903, making the eighty-mile journey from Darjeeling and after a week's travelling coming over the 14,400 feet pass of the Jelep La, to see before her the Promised Land:

A long deep valley stretches almost due north and south below our feet, its hollow bristling with black pines, parted by the white streak of a foaming, snow-fed stream. Closing the vista in the hazy blue distance there shoots up one single, dazzling sugar-loaf peak, the beautiful Chumularhi (about 25,000 feet). In the middle distance the picturesque group of the buildings and trees of the Kachu monastery nestle on a spur of the western valley wall.

But we must turn from this entrancing view to things nearer home. The climb down from the pass is indescribable, the worst part being, perhaps, the laborious descent of an hour over titanic boulders, toppling one upon the other and covered with a coating of glazed slush.

At the foot of this redoubtable descent lies the Chinese rest-house of Langrang. The way beyond is easier, despite stumbles over or in snow-covered stones and holes, and over the rudest of fenceless bridges continually crossing the brawling and swollen streams. Quite low down in the valley, while threading my way through the pink pine stems of a wood, I suddenly become aware of an advancing figure that exactly suits the surroundings. A brick-red gown of native cloth, with a glimpse of fawn silk at neck and wrists pouched up above the girdle, thus displaying blue cloth trousers tucked into fur boots the shape of night-socks, drapes a small person with a merry face, much too fair for a native, and topped by a yellow peaked cap. It is my sister! She greets me affectionately, asks if I have had a pleasant journey—much as if she were meeting me at Victoria Station—and takes me to the Mission House which has been her home since 1895.

Susette found 'a real attempt at cosiness', the ceiling was papered with the *Weekly Times* ('hard to beat for solidity') the walls were hung with patterned calico, a barometer, a wall clock and pictures, a samovar presented by 'a Russian officer and his wife' stood on a table, primulas in pots, books and ornaments were everywhere—the little parlour was, we can well believe, often crowded with visitors.

Annie was still at Yatung when the Younghusband Mission passed through in 1904 on its slow way to Lhasa, in an attempt to rationalize once and for all British relations with Tibet. She was also still carrying on a feud with authority. In correspondence exhumed from old Government files and quoted by Peter Fleming in his *Bayonets to Lhasa*, Miss Taylor makes a brisk and bizarre appearance, accusing the Commissioner of Customs of doing down his own countrymen in the interests of his Chinese paymasters and (surely a flight of fancy) of 'drowning his illegitimate children in my well'. She worked for a time as a nurse at the expedition's base camp in the Chumbi valley beyond Yatung, leaving Pontso and his wife to run the store. In 1907 a brother and sister-in-law visited her, and at different times she was joined by lady missionaries for short intervals. But the strain began to tell, and at some date before 1909 she went home in poor health.

I have not been able to discover the end of Annie's story. One hopes she found a 'Lhasa Villa' to retire to where her family could visit her; one hopes that Pontso wrote her the news from Tibet, and that perhaps she was godmother to Pontso's children. One can be sure she regretted no moment of her strange and adventurous life.

VI

Kate Marsden
1859–1931

From Whinny-muir when thou may'st pass,
　—*Every night and alle,*
To Brig o' Dread thou com'st at last;
　And Christe receive thy saule.

If ever thou gavest meat or drink,
　—*Every night and alle,*
The fire sall never make thee shrink;
　And Christe receive thy saule.

　　　　　　　The lykewake dirge, ANON.

On sledge and horseback to outcast Siberian lepers is the horrific title
of Kate Marsden's book, evoking a composite picture of
Florence Nightingale, David Livingstone and Albert Schweitzer
which is by no means wide of the mark. Miss Marsden was a
trained nurse on the Nightingale model, and she had all the
ardour of the dedicated medical missionary. Self-sacrifice was
the spur, and obsessive religious fervour the inspiration, which
drove her to seek in the forests of north-eastern Siberia the
forsaken lepers of Yakut.

Kate Marsden was born on 13 May, 1859 in what was then
the village of Edmonton, among the fields and orchards of
Middlesex where, as much as half a century later, Londoners
still followed John Gilpin in quest of holiday refreshment. Her
father was a prosperous solicitor with an office in Gilpin's own
Cheapside. Her mother is cryptically described by Kate's
biographer as 'a woman in whom the gentleness of her sex was
strongly developed, combined with strict ideas of family
discipline'. One is left wondering whether Mrs. Nickleby or
Miss Murdstone predominated. Outwardly the Marsdens were

a typical middle-class Victorian family, comfortable without being indecently wealthy, secluded behind the garden walls of their spacious suburban residence. Below the surface there were stresses. A family tradition of ill health weighed upon them, and they were haunted by the clammy spectre of consumption. So many deaths had there been in the family circle that the young Marsdens resolved never to marry, and before Kate was forty, tuberculosis had claimed all but herself and one brother. Perhaps a further breath of tragedy as well as of adventure was brought into the well-ordered home by the memory of the children's uncle, James Wellsted, who travelled in Arabia in the 1830's and died young after an attempt at suicide caused by protracted fever in distant desert lands.

Kate was the youngest of a family of eight and, as so often happens, the odd one out. While her sisters conformed to the pattern laid down for them, plying their needles and ful-filling their social obligations, she preferred carpentry and tree-climbing, and her practical curiosity landed her in such unladylike situations as being stuck in the greenhouse chimney while she investigated the heating system. Her dislike of lessons and resentment of schoolroom routine, the infinite boredom with which she regarded attempts to amuse her with fairy-stories, were only equalled by her horror of needlework. Her mother's 'strict ideas of family discipline' seem to have im-planted in the lively, lovable girl, with her original notions and heartfelt enthusiasms, a conviction of her own guilt in liking animals and flowers so much better than sums and sewing. Fortunately, she adored her dolls, an acceptable interest for a Victorian child, and her proficiency in nursing was acknowledged as useful and seemly.

Kate's father died when she was in her teens. The 'cleverness and integrity' attributed to him by her biographer do not seem to have stood him in very good stead, for he left his family ill provided for and the Edmonton house had to be sold. Mrs. Marsden, confronted with 'a sudden change from affluence to comparative poverty' turned to her growing-up family for support, and Kate's energy and practical talents were called into play. She decided to become a nurse, a career only very recently made possible for girls of good family by the great Florence Nightingale, whose own school of nursing at St.

Thomas's was founded in 1860. Kate was accepted for training at the Tottenham hospital, then at Snell's Park, near her old home in Edmonton. The Prince of Wales's General Hospital, as it has been called since 1893, developed out of the Ragged School founded in Tottenham in 1855 by the Jewish doctor Michael Laseron, who had left Germany to settle in England when he became a Christian and was cold-shouldered in his home town. The school flourished with a fine Evangelical fervour, and before long grew into an orphanage for 800 girls with an infirmary attached. In 1867 a Deaconess from the famous Lutheran Institute at Kaiserwerth began training some of the older girls to work among the sick poor in Tottenham. Out of this small beginning grew the Evangelical Deaconesses' Institute which, in 1883, moved into new premises on The Green, just off Tottenham High Road, where it is today. The Institute owed its origin and success to two people—Laseron himself, who lived to a good old age as a kind of local saint, and Lady Christian Dundas, the Superintendent, a loved and familiar figure in the black bonnet and shawl which were the uniform of her mother-house at Kaiserwerth. The Tottenham Community was conceived as an Evangelical counterpart to the Roman Catholic Nursing sisterhoods. No binding vows were exacted—that would have been too like Popery—but there was strong moral pressure on the women and girls who came for training to regard their vocation as life-long, and they received no salary. Nor was nursing the only concern at Tottenham. A reporter from *The Queen*, visiting the hospital's new premises in 1885, not many years after Kate finished her training, described the texts on the walls, the tracts on the tables and the prayers in the wards, and claimed that 'the occupation of nursing is as yet secondary to the main purpose of the deaconesses' life; its thoughts and intentions are directed to the conversion of souls'. Hymn singing and scripture study were part of the daily routine of the wards, and the minds of out-patients were taken off their ailments by Bible reading and impromptu services. Workers of all denominations were welcomed provided they were within the Evangelical fold; what would the pious founders have thought of the spiritual arrangements at the Prince of Wales's Hospital today, which include the appointment of Roman Catholic as well as Anglican and

Annie Taylor and Pontso.

Mary Kingsley's canoe on the Ogowé.
'A lady an explorer? A traveller in skirts?'

Annie Taylor, '*a figure that exactly suits the surroundings.*'

Mary Kingsley in 1895; she considered one had '*no right to go about Africa in things one would be ashamed of at home.*'

'*When we come to clothes, our travellers appear at their most remarkable.*'

Free Church Chaplains to minister to staff and patients?

Besides being missionaries first and nurses second, the deaconesses were social workers and the new building included a Mission Hall where they held Sunday schools, Bible classes, mothers' meetings, and temperance meetings; they ran a library and a penny bank. 'The religious services are conducted with little or no ceremonial; the whole life led in the institution is simple, earnest, practical' rejoiced the writer in *The Queen*, who went on to extol the 'peaceful, simple, busy home where is gathered in voluntary bond a community of women whose Christianity is active and primitive.' Kate spent less than a year at Tottenham, eight years before these impressions were published, but the atmosphere is likely to have been much the same from the first. She was young, impressionable and eager, offering an uncommitted personality to the dynamic impact of Victorian Evangelical enthusiasm. The impression on her was indelible, and very like the effect on Annie Taylor of the China Inland Mission. In both cases energies which had caused friction at home and, where Kate was concerned, induced feelings of guilt and frustration, were harnessed to a cause. In Annie's case, they were satisfactorily harnessed for life; in Kate's, a less stable nervous system may even have been damaged by the intensity of the religious atmosphere in which she felt so immediately at home.

Sister Christian's devotion to local needs, the love and zeal with which she fired the workers she was not allowed to compel, was equalled by the breadth of vision which sent the Tottenham nurses out into the world, as far afield as the battlefields of Serbia and the Catholic strongholds of Cork and Dublin. Contingents of nurses tended the wounded in several Balkan wars in the seventies, and in the Franco-Prussian War; they were also welcomed to nurse the Protestant patients in the Cork Infirmary and in the South Dublin Union where one of them so far disarmed religious prejudice as to become Matron. It was this international aspect of the work that appealed to Kate, and great was her delight when in 1877 she was allowed to join a party of nurses going to Bulgaria to tend Russian soldiers wounded in the Russo-Turkish War. She had only eight months training behind her, but she had been, according to Sister Christian, 'an intelligent, willing pupil' with 'decided nursing talent and ability'. That she had always 'assisted vigorously in nursing the sick Sisters' may have decided the Superintendent to send her to look after the older members of the party who were probably glad of a keen and devoted young girl to do the routine jobs. That Sister Christian also commended Kate for being 'very kind to the patients' during her training is a reminder that the amusing legend of Sarah Gamp was, in 1877, still something of an ugly reality. Nothing survives of Kate's experiences in Bulgaria but a passing reference by Henry Johnson, the biographer of her early years, to travelling in 'strong, rough waggons, with straw for cushions', and the information that it was here she first became interested in leprosy, and aware of an increasingly urgent call to care for lepers. Sent out from camp with a companion to search for any wounded who might have been overlooked on the battlefield, she made her way into a deserted barn. Inside she found two men suffering from leprosy, scarcely recognizable as human beings. The experience was traumatic; its awful impact on the sensitive mind and soul of the young girl was never forgotten. For the time being, however, it lay dormant and she returned to England to take up a conventional nursing career, first at the Westminster Hospital and later as Sister-in-Charge of the Woolton Convalescent Home at Liverpool. She stayed there for four and a half years, her satisfaction in the work much enhanced by the mixture of nationalities she had to deal with in this big seaport town. When she resigned owing to ill health (lung trouble, the family bogey, was feared), she received a blaze of grateful testimonials, a cheque for £100 and 'a handsome tricycle'.

In 1884 she and her mother went to New Zealand to see the last of an invalid sister of Kate's who had hoped to find a cure on the other side of the world, and was now dying of consumption. Kate, herself much better in health, took a post as Lady Superintendent of Wellington Hospital where she put into practice all she had learnt at Tottenham of practical nursing and constructive social work. Her 'cheeriness', we are told, made a great impression on the 'rough miners' who were brought into the hospital after accidents in the mines; she started first-aid classes, and rallied the New Zealand ladies to form a branch of St. John's Ambulance Brigade. But a happy and useful career was soon disastrously interrupted. What the 'severe accident' was that she met with at Wellington Hospital, her biographer does not say, but 'for several months she was dangerously ill' with 'a most trying mental illness'. She herself refers to 'the period when I took many backward steps and turned away from Christ', and one must assume that she had a serious nervous breakdown, accompanied probably by a kind of revulsion against the intense religious training of her youth. There is a suggestion of a guilt complex, a desire to atone for something, in the intensity with which on her recovery she decided to devote herself to the cause of the world's lepers— she even hoped to discover a cure. For with returning sanity came also a revival of the concern which had imprinted itself on her mind thirteen years before in the haunted barn on the half-forgotten Bulgarian battlefield. She returned to England, fully restored to health, and when, in 1890, she was invited to St. Petersburg to receive a medal from the Russian Red Cross, she made this a starting point for an exhaustive enquiry into the lot of lepers, not only in Russia but in the Near and Middle East; she decided, too to visit hospitals in Paris and to discuss the problem with Pasteur. Convinced that only by having friends in high places could she penetrate to the heart of the leprosy problem, she applied to be presented at Court and attended a Drawing-Room on 5 March 1890. This led to her being received by the Princess of Wales who gave her a personal introduction to the Empress of Russia and, armed with this, Kate stormed the social and official worlds of St. Petersburg and Moscow.

There must have been a magnetism and urgency about her personality which are not conveyed by the stilted phrases of Johnson's *Life of Kate Marsden*. We are told of her 'stately appearance' in her 'nurse's garb', of her 'clever way of blending humour with instruction' and, more than once, of her 'cheeriness'. An image obstinately obtrudes of one of those unbearable jolly nurses who enter the ward crying 'How are we?' The real Kate Marsden, who charmed the Tsarina and her ladies-in-waiting and blasted her way through the embattled bureaucracy of Imperial Russia must have been a very different and infinitely more impressive figure. That she made her mark in Royal and official circles is due also to the fact, more acceptable in Victorian times than today, that she was a philanthropist and not a reformer. She desired passionately to help the unfortunate; she was very little concerned with altering their condition in life. Kate would have joined as heartily as any other member of a clean, well-ordered Victorian congregation in the singing of Mrs. Alexander's popular hymn:

> The rich man in his castle,
> The poor man at the gate;
> God made them high or lowly,
> And ordered their estate.

When my own grandmother ventured to pity the lot of the crossing sweeper to whom my grandfather gave half-a-crown every Sunday on the way to church, she was told: 'He is as well off in his station as I am in mine'—there is the best and worst of our immediate ancestors in a nutshell, and a point of view Kate would have shared. When later she visited the prisons and leper settlements of Europe she had none of the dedicated reformer's indignation at the lot of the inmates but (what was perhaps more immediately useful) more than the ordinary philanthropist's compulsion to make that lot more bearable. She can speak of 'a charming leper colony' and 'a splendid prison' without trace of irony, being well endowed with 'cheeriness' but not at all with the subleties of humour in which her contemporary Mary Kingsley, for instance, excelled.

Kate set herself now to organize her 'roving commission to hunt up lepers wherever she had an inkling of their existence'. All the practical curiosity of her youth, all the warm-hearted compassion of her adolescence, found direction and at the age of thirty she was ready for her mission. She visited Jerusalem and Constantinople and made her way back to Moscow by way of the Caucasus; it was in Tiflis she had her attention drawn to the Siberian lepers who seemed to be uncared for beyond the worst plight of any of the sufferers in Middle Eastern lands or overseas. Kate was an optimist and she was given additional enthusiasm for her self-imposed task by hearing that in Siberia grew one of the many herbs which, in the days when much was hoped from the herbal treatment of leprosy, it was thought might yield a cure. Modern treatment has superseded such remedies, but Siberian leprosy was a real enough scourge, and in November 1890 she arrived in Moscow ready to proceed, after obtaining the necessary permits, for the northern wilds.

Siberia in the 1890's was, as Miss Marsden explains, 'a place principally for prisoners and officials'; there were also in the remote Viluisk Circuit rather less than 100 lepers, expelled from their villages to drag out a living death in filthy huts, the diseased, dying and dead huddled together in the freezing cold of the northern forests. It was Kate's plan, after her preliminary work in whipping up interest in Russia and in England, and collecting money, simply to go to Siberia and find out for herself what needed to be done. She was no armchair philanthropist. She spoke no Russian and officials in Moscow and St. Petersburgh were understandably puzzled and suspicious— she was even suspected of being a spy, but with the Empress's backing she obtained the necessary permission and left Moscow on 1 February 1891 with a Russian speaking friend, Miss Anna Field.

In 1891 the Trans-Siberian Railway was only a blue-print; transport beyond the Urals was largely provided by sledges, to be hired with driver and horses for a standard fee. 'Bumping, jolting, tossing; heaved, pitched and thumped. Bright memories of asphalt, blockwood, and penny omnibuses spring up to diversify your thoughts.' This was their progress over hard-frozen roads, churned up by the heavy traffic on its way to the great February fair at Irbit. As night fell the eyes of wolves twinkled through the dense wayside trees. Drivers might be drunk or incompetent, and the public rest-houses seem to have been far less comfortable than Fanny's station waiting-rooms in India. Closely shuttered against the bitter cold (the English ladies longed for a good draught of fresh air and Kate once broke the window to get one), there were insects creeping up the walls and the sheepskin rugs on the floor provided a communal sleeping place. The travellers boarded their first sledge at Zlatoust, not without difficulty owing to the immense amount of clothing worn against the cold. What with felt boots and leather overboots, eiderdown coats and sheepskin over-coats (to mention only the outer garments) 'three muscular policemen' were needed to heave Miss Marsden and her friend, weighed down like medieval knights in armour, into their conveyance. Weight of another kind was carried in the form of 'good, solid, old-English plum pudding', chosen as their staple diet, being palatable in all weathers and keeping indefinitely. Forty pounds of this 'delicious compound' were packed, with only a few boxes of sardines, biscuits, bread and tea in addition. And it was Miss Marsden's vehemently held belief that she owed her life 'humanly speaking' to abstinence from alcoholic stimulants and to Dr. Jaeger's Porous Woollen Clothing.

The journey from Zlatoust to Irkutsk in southern Siberia took three months in weather so cold that 'the icicles froze on my friend's veil'. Their last touch with civilization was Ekaterinburg where they found 'an excellent American hotel' (though, alas, the prison was 'not of the best'). From here they hurried on the hundred miles to Irbit hoping to meet at the fair merchants from the north who would give them first-hand news of the Yakut lepers. The stage from Irbit to Tjumen was 'the worst bit of sledging I ever experienced' not only because of the holes in the road and the hillocks of frozen snow, but for the impositions of 'a free driver, in distinction from Government drivers', who 'had some of the rights and privileges which the drivers of "private" omnibuses so provokingly assume'. At Tjumen Mr. and Mrs. Wardroper of the British and Foreign Bible Society gave them a 'hearty English welcome' and saw them off to Tobolsk.

> The horses dashed off full gallop, rushing through freshly formed snowdrifts. The snow soon found its way into every corner of the sledge, which, although covered at the top, was quite open in front. Then the snow had a way of settling down the collars of our coats, and, when melted by the heat of the body, trickling down the neck; and sometimes it flew up the sleeves unless we were careful to keep them closed at the wrists. Our good substantial boxes were all stowed away in the 'hold'; over them was a layer of straw, and on the straw we sat, or, rather reclined, with pillows at our backs. The word 'reclined' suggests ease and comfort; but when applied to sledge-travelling, under the circumstances that we travelled, it means 'Hobson's choice.' You are compelled to put yourself, or get put into that position; and in that position you must remain . . .
>
> For six hours all went well, with the normal amount of bumping and jolting. We had, this time, another youthful driver, a rare specimen of 'young Siberia'. As darkness fell it appeared to us that he was getting a little reckless; but we said nothing,

attributing his daring exploits to vodka, or to the bitter cold, or to the faulty way of harnessing the horses. Anyhow, as midnight approached, it must be confessed that we became slightly nervous and irritable, having our recent nocturnal adventure vividly before our minds. We had a strong presentiment that something was going to happen. The harness, I must mention, is often responsible for accidents in sledge travelling . . .

I was thinking of the two outer horses, and speculating how soon the horses' legs would get entangled in the odds and ends of rope that were supposed to help in keeping the horses together, when suddenly the second horse disappeared! The driver gave a lurch forward; the off-horse struggled; there was a bump and a thump against the sledge, and then the other horse also disappeared, and we came to a deadlock. We were both wide-awake in no time and we heard and felt an ominous knocking against the side; and on looking out we found both horses entangled in the ropes and on the ground, struggling frantically to get up.

The driver called 'Nichevo' (It is nothing). But no amount of 'nichevoeing' prevented my feeling uneasy . . . I got my friend to translate a rather peremptory order to both men; and this woke them up to the fact that they must be doing something besides abusing each other . . . The soldier quickly stood on one horse's neck, and the driver set the harness free. The other animal was treated in the same way; but the driver was evidently too angry with it to drive it any more; and so he just let it loose and away it trotted, looking such an odd creature in the half snowlight, with the harness dragging all around it. The oddity of the scene made us enjoy a hearty laugh, notwithstanding the discomfort of the occasion. After a little more hard tugging and painful compulsion, the three remaining horses were put, or rather tied, together, and away we started again.

But no sooner were they on their way again that they ran full tilt into a heavy freight sledge and were decanted into a ditch, struggling out only to lose their way. First they careered over a ploughed field and then slid down a steep hill to pull up short on the brink of a frozen river. Kate's famous cheeriness stood her in good stead: 'We expected another catastrophe every moment, and hardly knew whether to laugh or to cry. We chose the former alternative and merrily awaited events.'

As they pressed on into Siberia they came on gangs of convicts tramping hopelessly along under guards, and each town had its prison. Trained to miss no opportunity of ministering

to those in need, Kate carried a supply of New Testaments and
of little packets of tea and sugar to be distributed to the dis-
pirited parties met on the road. She also visited the gaols which
varied from the 'splendid prison' at Tobolsk to a 'black hole'
at Kansk, insanitary and unventilated, and so dark that only
the rattling of chains told her that it was full of manacled men.
She and Miss Field moved freely among these unfortunates,
quite unafraid and only coming away when the foul air over-
came them—'I giving tea and sugar and the little Gospels and
my friend speaking of the Word of Life.' Once the onset of a
snow-storm reminded her she had heard of a gang on the road
ahead, and she hurried forward to give them the tea which
might warm them a little; once she was told that the prison was
closing for the night and she pushed past the guards into darkness only lit by the stub of a candle, stumbling as she went over
the bodies crowded two deep on the filthy floor. 'Perhaps some
friends might think that this trifling attention to the physical
needs of the prisoners was superfluous, and that I ought to have
been contented with spiritual ministration. But I asked myself,
I hope not presumptiously, what would Christ have done? And
I felt that He would first attend in some degree to the material
wants of such outcasts before offering the Bread of Life.' Such
passages should remind the reader that baiting the Victorians
is, after all, a trivial sport.

At Omsk poor Miss Field had to give up, and beyond Tomsk
travelling became dangerous with the spring thaw. The slushy,
shifting surface of the great river Yenissei brought her heart
into her mouth but like Annie Taylor by the flooded Hwang-
Ho she trusted to the Lord to bring her over in safety. At
Krasnoyarsk (which boasted an 'excellent prison') she changed
from an uncomfortable sledge into a Little-ease of a wheeled
vehicle called a tarantass, and then after three weeks by boat
on the river Lena she arrived in Yakutsk, a dreary town shuttered most of the year against the cold where the inhabitants
spent most of their time indoors, smoking and playing cards.
She visited the Bishop, and was much impressed by his holy
demeanour. Might not this godly man, one wonders, have done
something himself for the afflicted souls in his diocese, instead of
leaving it all to his valiant Englishwoman? Ever since 1827
correspondence had been going on between various official

bodies about the lepers' plight; by a single courageous resolution Kate was to cut through this tangle of red tape but, typically, she does not seem to have resented the tape being there—she was highly gratified by the Bishop's blessing.

Backed by a committee of the leading men in Yakutsk Kate left for Viluisk on 22 June 1891, with an escort of fifteen men led by the Cossack Jean Procopieff who had been so impressed by her enthusiasm that he had provided free of charge the thirty horses needed for the 1,000 mile ride. Unlike Isabella, Kate was quite inexperienced as a horsewoman, the ponies were wild and the saddles of heavy wood; she shared Isabella's doubts of the propriety of riding astride. 'I rather shrink from giving a description of my costume,' she confessed, 'because it was so inelegant. I wore a jacket, with very long sleeves, and had the badge of the red cross on my left arm. Then I had to wear full trousers to the knees. The hat was an ordinary deerstalker, which I had bought in London. I carried a whip, and a little travelling bag, slung over the shoulder.' The days of cold and dark, of stifling rooms and suffocating smoke were over; mosquitoes and bears, broiling heat and thunderstorms, forest fires and quaking bogs, nights spent in the open—these were the lot of Kate and her Cossack escort. Already tired out by the journey to Yakutsk, she arrived in Viluisk shaking with exhaustion, nauseated by the rough food and by the ravages of mosquitoes. Here Jean Procopieff handed her over to the care of the Viliusk authorities; hardly waiting to rest she summoned a committee and picked out as her right-hand man the priest Father John Vinokouroff, one of the few people who could bring himself to approach the lepers.

It is easy to make fun of much of Kate's *On sledge and horseback*, written, as much of it is, in a style reminiscent of those Victorian phrase books in which the postillion is struck by lightning and the chambermaid is drunk; the situations are often ludicrous and the opinions unsophisticated. But her descriptions of the lepers and what she tried to do for them are not amusing. Their lot was worse than anything she had been told or could have imagined. Here and there, a rough attempt had been made to gather them into some kind of settlement, which was no more than a hut or two crowded to suffocation by the living, the dying and often the dead, provisioned from the village dustbins; sometimes individual sufferers would be driven out to exist as best they might on scraps left for them in the snow. There were men and women, with limbs eaten away, hardly able to crawl to fetch their food; there were children, sometimes undiseased but condemned to stay with their leper parents, sometimes driven from their homes to die in the forest lest they should contaminate the whole family; for most of the year the cold was so relentless than for days on end the lepers could not leave their horrible shacks even to bury their dead. Kate did not take the stories she heard on trust. She arranged journeys into the forest to see for herself, which were to take her another 1,000 miles even more dangerously and uncomfortably than the ride from Yakutsk. She was accompanied by the local inspector of police, or *ispravnick*, and four village elders, and 'about twenty Yakuts, all mounted on horseback . . . The wild, ungroomed, unkempt horses added to the singularity of the scene.' The local people had cut a road through the forest for the party, or it is doubtful if she would ever have got through. Paths over the swamps were marked by poles, and a trail blazed through the woods with a mark on a tree at every twenty yards. Although little or nothing had been done for the lepers in all the years they had been there, Kate's coming seems to have galvanized the local authorities in an extraordinary way and nothing was too much trouble for them. They led her along the treacherous, weary paths, the horses stumbling over dead roots or sinking to the hocks in marshy ground, dismounting only to take to an unsteady boat on a river lashed by a storm.

We wended our way through the forest along the 1,500 verst track that the Yakuts had so readily and lovingly marked for us; for they did this work of their own will and without remuneration, though to accomplish it they had to lay aside their summer work in the fields. They knew whither we were bound, and this was the proof of their sympathy for the mission and their pity for the lepers.

Although the path had been marked out for us, the stumps and roots of trees had been left. We rode over a carpet of half-decayed roots, all interlaced with one another. Now and then my horse sank, not this time in mud, but into holes, well hidden amongst the roots, getting his feet entangled in such a way that only a Siberian horse could extricate himself. I had to hang on to the saddle, my body ready for every lurch the horse might give in freeing himself, and prepared to help him at the right moment. We went through miles and miles of forest like this.

At last I thought I could discern ahead a large lake, and beyond that two yourtas [huts]. My instinct was true to me; and the peculiar thrill which passed through my whole frame meant that, at last, after all those months of travelling, I had found, thank God! the poor creatures whom I had come to help. A little more zigzag riding along the tedious path, and then I suddenly looked up and saw before me the two yourtas and a little crowd of people. Some of the people came limping, and some leaning on sticks, to catch the first glimpse of us, their faces and limbs distorted by the dreadful ravages of the disease. One poor creature could only crawl by help of a stool, and all had the same indescribably hopeless expression of the eyes which indicates the disease. I scrambled off the horse, and went quickly amongst the little crowd of the lame, the halt, and the blind. Some were standing, some were kneeling, and some crouching on the ground, and all with eager faces turned towards me. They told me afterwards that they believed God had sent me; and, my friends, if you could all have been there, you would no longer wonder at my having devoted body and soul to this work.

I at once ordered the things to be unpacked, and had them collected on the grass. A prayer of thanksgiving was then offered by the priest, and next, a prayer for her Imperial Majesty the Empress, in which the poor people heartily joined. As we distributed the gifts, some of the distorted faces half beamed with delight; whilst others changed from a look of fear to one of confidence and rest. Surely such a scene was worth a long journey, and many hardships and perils.

Kate soon sorted out a girl who, though not a leper, had lived in these fearful conditions for eighteen years with her mother, who had been driven from the village as a leper before the girl was born. Kate's influence was such that the Inspector of Police offered to take the girl home as a servant and was indeed as good as his word. On the return from this expedition to Viluisk, Kate collapsed from exhaustion, but twenty-four hours' complete rest set her up for another and longer tour. She moved among the lepers fearlessly, with her gifts of tea and sugar, her Gospels and her message of earthly hope. She watched, deeply moved, while Father John administered Holy Communion to a pathetic group of outcasts; as a Protestant she could not join actively in the service, but her prayers were fervent. Plans for a colony were discussed and possible sites inspected; one committee meeting, in the half-light of the northern summer night, culminated in a picnic at midnight which proved 'a light and innocent little diversion from the serious business that weighed upon our minds'. By boat and on horseback, on foot and once even carried by her escort she covered in all some thousand miles. They were threatened by bears, and sometimes the ground shook under their feet with subterranean fire:

We had been travelling for about twenty miles since leaving the last place, when I noticed how strangely the horses' tread sounded—just as if they were walking over a tunnel, with only a shallow roof to it. The tchinovnick explained that this was one of the places where the earth was in a state of combustion. The fire begins a long way below the surface, and burns slowly, still more slowly when there is no vent for the smoke. The burnt earth creates great hollows, and there is always danger of a horse breaking the crust and sinking into the fire. I thought little more about the matter except speculating on the causes of this alarming phenomenon in the bosom of Mother Earth.

Night came on, and all was gloom around us. By and by I thought I saw in the distance several lights; going on a little farther the lights became a glare, and then my horse became restive and almost unmanageable. We emerged from the forest and stood in an open space. What an unearthly scene met my eyes! The whole earth, not the forest, for miles around seemed full of little flickers of fire; flames of many colours—red, gold, blue, and purple—darted up on every hand, some forked and jagged, some straight as a javelin, rising here and there above the earth, and, in places, seeming to lick the dust, and then, having gained fresh energy, springing as high as the others . . . Coming, full of nervous apprehension, out of the dark forest on to such a scene, I half fancied that those flames were endowed with life. The lurid spectacle looked like a high carnival of curious creatures, let loose for a time from the prison-house, careering about in fantastic shapes. Blinding clouds of smoke every now and then swept into our eyes, and the hot stifling air almost choked us.

We had to go through the fire; there was no escaping it, unless we chose to turn back. After looking on, aghast, for some time, and trying to prevent our terrified horses from bolting, we moved slowly forward, picking our way as best we could in and out of the flames. I prepared, as well as I was able, for any emergency, slipping my feet to the edge of the stirrups in order to release myself in case of an accident, then tightened the reins, and followed my guide . . .

Soon we entered a splendid forest; and coming from vivid light into darkness, the darkness to me was blackness indeed. My horse kept stumbling, and first one branch and then another hit me in the face. I again dropped the reins on to the horse's neck, put up my arms to shield my face, and left all in God's hands. As my eyes grew accustomed to the pitchy gloom I could see the white tip of my dog's tail. I quite forgot to mention this faithful friend before. He was an ordinary black collie, with a white tail. I knew that he always followed the Yakut guide, who rode in front of me; so I kept my eyes fixed on that little bit of white, and felt that, as long as I could see it, I was tolerably safe; if the white spot disappeared I knew we were near a hole, and so must be prepared for an accident.

Complete physical exhaustion came at last. I had never been on a horse before, except once, for a short time, several years ago; and after all these weeks of riding on a hard saddle, with little sleep and food, and all the perils and alarms of the journey— well, it was time, perhaps the reader may think, that I did get exhausted. So I had to rest, and I began to feel symptoms of an internal malady, which at first alarmed me; and I thought I might have to die there in my little tent, and leave, only just commenced, all the work I wanted to do. But the Master's presence cheered me and banished all depression. A day's rest, and then I started again, although in great pain, which, unfortunately, lasted till the end of the journey.

Kate rode back to Yakutsk in stages of seventy miles a day, nagged by severe pain and so weak she tied the reins to her wrists and let the horse have its head. Finally the escort commandeered a cart and laid her on a rough bed of straw—'like a wounded soldier after battle', she commented, thinking perhaps of the Bulgarian campaign and the errands of mercy of her youth. The journey home was a repetition of the one out, only she was less able to bear it, covered as she was in cuts and bruises, suffering internal pain, ill-fed and utterly exhausted. She was not, however, so defeated as not to be able to stand up to an extortionate driver on the long trek by tarantass from Irkutsk to Tomsk. Pay the price of seven horses for four she would not, 'holding up four fingers' until 'hoarse muttering gradually succeeded to the shouting, and at last I got four horses at their proper price'—'it is astonishing the effect that English coolness has on the Russian temper.' Indeed, it was Miss Marsden's considered opinion that if only English or American enterprise could be set to work in Siberia the place would be much improved and developed, the Siberians themselves being a thoroughly good, and improvable, sort of people, very like English colonials in temperament. Miss Field met her at Tjumen, and nursed her back—if not to health at least to a state when she could continue the journey without danger. When they reached Zlatoust her nerves were so weak that she felt 'a curious fit of emotion' on seeing again a railway station and trains, and was seized with 'glee and excitement'. She was back in Moscow by December where she attended a meeting of the Venereological and Dermatological Society. Her report on her journey was read, and a hospital was built later, staffed by nuns and paid for by the proceeds of her own writing and lectures, and begged from everyone from the Empress downwards, in Russia, England and America. Contemporary Russian accounts give 32,000 roubles as the sum which went to the founding of the hospital opened at Viluisk in 1897. Accommodation for patients was arranged in six separate buildings, with a six-roomed doctor's house, a laboratory and a library in addition. The hospital throve, admitting its maximum of seventy-six patients in 1902, twenty years after Kate's journey. By 1917, the numbers had fallen to nineteen, and they continued to fall up to a few years ago when the hospital was closed, having accomplished its purpose. Kate's valiant work was warmly acknowledged in the Russia of her day. An anonymous account of her journey was published in Russian in Moscow in 1892, and in 1904 the author of a monograph on leprosy, D. F. Reshitillo, paid her a tribute:

> Miss Marsden fully deserves her name to be mentioned in the history of leprosy in Siberia. One must pay full justice to her rare energy, and to the unusual degree of self-denial essential for a young woman who did not know Russian to overcome the incredible difficulties of a journey in Siberia in order to reach the so-called 'dead places' to which the lepers were banished; to observe in detail and describe everything concerning the lepers; to return, to put the Russian society on its feet; to collect the

necessary funds in a foreign land, and virtually to settle the destiny of the leprous Yakuts.

That she is not forgotten in the very different Russia of our own time is shown by the fact that whereas there is no record of the results of her mission in this country, I was able to learn by return of post these details about her and the Viliusk hospital from a Soviet authority on leprosy, Professor N. Torsuev.

She staged an exhibit at the Chicago World Fair and in 1893 published *On sledge and horseback*. Details are lacking of the darker side of the picture, the persecution which she declares she suffered and which led her to publish in 1921 *My mission to Siberia: A vindication*. Apparently doubts were cast on her veracity as a traveller and on her integrity as an administrator; even her sanity was questioned and her breakdown in New Zealand ill-naturedly remembered. The Royal Geographical Society, however, had no doubts about her claims as a traveller and included her in the group of 'well-qualified ladies' elected in 1892. She took great pride in this, even though she was refused a ticket to the Annual Dinner. There were compensations for this and other vexations: Queen Victoria gave her a gold brooch in the form of an angel, now in the R.G.S. Museum, and in 1906 she attended a Court although she had already been presented once—a sure indication of status. The *Geographical Journal* praised the authenticity of her book, the reviewer, who had been in Siberia, particularly commending the description of the subterranean fire which I have quoted. In 1916 she was nominated a Free Life Fellow of the R.G.S., a rare distinction.

The collection of funds and the promotion of publicity on behalf of the hospital kept her busy for the next few years. Kate Marsden never travelled again, her health having been irremediably damaged by all she had gone through, and her plan to visit lepers in Kamchatka came to nothing. She died in 1931 at Hillingdon, Middlesex after thirty years of invalid life, and her friend Miss Norris presented to the R.G.S. the watch and whistle Kate had used in Siberia. Miss Norris also gave the Society a large framed photograph of Miss Marsden in Court dress, signed by her and dated 1906, which was placed, appropriately enough, in the Ladies' Smoking Room.

PART FIVE

The Voyager

VII

Mary Kingsley
1862–1900

And find, when fighting shall be done,
Great rest, and fullness after dearth.
Into Battle, JULIAN GRENFELL

MARY Kingsley is the joker in the pack. True, her stout
Victorian skirt and prim head-dress, the umbrella with which
she prodded hippopotami and took marine soundings, seem to
identify her with the conventionally unconventional sisterhood
whose adventures I have tried to record. She shares with them
also a courage and integrity which carried her round many
tight corners and allowed her to come pretty close to pitch
without defilement. But the quality of her intellect was unique,
her political judgement strikingly sophisticated and informed;
her opinions, founded on rational thinking, were her own and
little influenced by current fashion. Could Memsahib Fanny,
scolding her coolies up the glaciers, have said as Miss Kingsley
said of the cannibal Fans: 'We each recognized that we belonged to that same section of the human race with whom it is
better to drink than to fight?' Can one imagine Isabella Bird
championing the liquor trade? And the mind refuses to admit
the idea of Kate Marsden in Mary's predicament: 'When I
and the captain of a vessel had to take to the saloon table because a Bishop with a long red beard and voluminous white
flannel petticoats was rolling about the floor in close but warful
embrace with the Governor of the Ogowé, utterly deaf to the
messages of peace the Captain and I poured down on them.'

Mary Kingsley's fame today rests to a large extent on her
pioneer work in the anthropological field and in her champion-
ship of causes which have now fallen into perspective as part of

Africa's stormy political history. As a traveller, she is apt to be regarded in a faintly comic light, and qualities which her contemporaries well understood are often ignored—her amazing courage and cleverness, her unique capacity for bizarre adventures in a quest for equally bizarre information. Though she disclaimed any primary interest in geography, and anticipated modern exploration in being more concerned with the intensive study of a small and unfrequented region than with tracing long routes on a known map, she had an uncanny knack of finding her way over difficult country. And in her acute observation of natural phenomena she equals the great Livingstone himself. Like him, she had many facets. She was a naturalist and an ethnologist, a scholar and a sailor, as well as a champion of lost causes, a faithful daughter and sister, a beloved friend. In the old-fashioned headings in which she summarizes the chapters in *Travels in West Africa*, she calls herself 'the voyager', and it is in this capacity she was happiest and most completely fulfilled. It is, of course, as a voyager that she appears in these pages, gay, gallant and shockingly tough, as impervious to discomfort and danger for herself as to the fears of the lesser mortals she drew into her tearing slip-stream. At the same time, she had a poetic sensitivity to the call of the wild which recalls Emily Brontë—who would probably have been equally indifferent to the commonplace amenities of hot baths, clean sheets and new clothes. Isabella Bird made her a present of a beautiful Chinese dress which she refused to wear as being too fine.

Mary Kingsley was born on 13 October 1862 and the first thirty years of her life were restricted beyond what was normal even for a Victorian girl of good family. She spent a week in Paris in her early twenties, otherwise her horizon was bounded by a home where her father was often away, her mother often ill and her brother always ineffective. Mary was the man of the house, keeping a series of rather ramshackle homes in order with the help of a 'delightful paper' called *The English Mechanic*, rearing gamecocks by way of a hobby and reading everything she could lay hands on in her father's library. She inherited a passion for travel and an unquenchable vitality from this father, a younger brother of the more famous Charles. George Kingsley was a restless, eccentric man who read much and travelled widely, leaving in his daughter's mind an ideal of manhood untarnished by the self-indulgence which kept him wandering round the world, leaving his wife in England, often anxious and always lonely, to bring up Mary and her brother Charles in various homes of which the last was at Cambridge, where they moved when Mary was twenty-two. She was largely self-taught with a taste for science and an aptitude for the practical application of knowledge; a course in German, which she learnt in order to help her father in his study of native religions, was the only part of her education which cost a penny. When her parents died within a few weeks of each other in 1892 she was left suddenly with no purpose in life, so she determined to try and complete her father's unfinished anthropological work. George Kingsley had travelled among the islanders of the Pacific and the Indians of North America, he had studied deeply the ways and beliefs of the Chinese, the Indians, and the Semitic peoples; Africa was a gap in his knowledge which his daughter determined to fill, and scientific friends suggested that if she was set on going to Africa she might while there study and collect freshwater fishes and other zoological specimens. 'Fish and fetish' is how she described the objects of going to 'skylark and enjoy myself in Africa', and after trying her wings on a trip to the Canary Isles she began to lay plans in all seriousness for her African adventures. In the event she learnt and collected far more than she had envisaged, becoming so passionately interested in all she saw that what began as an academic study developed into a practical crusade —a campaign to interpret all things West African and to break through the apathy and ignorance of her countrymen who were faced, at the turn of the century, with the responsibility of administering great tracts of the so-called 'Dark Continent', which the European Powers were carving up into 'spheres of influence'.

Her travels were all accomplished in the short interval between August 1893 and November 1895. The 'Scramble for Africa' was at its height, with the European Powers staking out claims east and west of the continent in the independent free-for-all which succeeded King Leopold's short-lived project for an International Association to open up Africa. When Mary landed in West Africa Leopold was firmly established in the

Congo Free State, which Stanley had been developing for him, and Portugal was sitting tight in her old stronghold of Angola. Britain, France and Germany were jostling each other along the coast and into the interior where the raw material of trade was to be tapped. Colonial responsibilities were a new, and unwelcome, commitment where the British Government were concerned, but there had been traders on the Coast for centuries, and it was in a Liverpool cargo boat that Mary first set sail. Her education as a 'Coaster' began on the voyage out, when her fellow passengers, traders to a man, entertained her with stories—dismal, macabre and comic—of the dangers and discomforts of the 'white man's grave'. They took her at first for a missionary with her drab clothes, gaunt figure and scraped-back hair, but were undeceived by her 'failure during a Sunday service in the Bay of Biscay, to rescue it from the dire confusion into which it had been thrown by an esteemed and able officer and a dutiful but inexperienced purser'. Brought up an agnostic, and unsympathetic to missions, Mary determined to travel as a trader, feeling that thus could she best gain the confidence of the bush Africans whose ways she had come to study. She carried the usual trade goods, principally cloth and tobacco with fish-hooks for small change, to offer against ivory and rubber, and she was accredited to the West Coast firm of Hatton and Cookson. She took pains to learn the technique and routine of trading and, nothing if not resourceful, once bartered twelve of her own blouses to get herself out of a dangerous spot, noting with interest their effect 'when worn by a brawny warrior with *nothing* else but red paint and a bunch of leopard tails'.

On her first journey she landed at St. Paul de Loanda, spent some time with the Fjort tribe on the Congo and travelled north through the Congo Free State, across the river into French territory and so to Old Calabar in the British sphere. She returned to England with a valuable collection of natural history specimens, selected and preserved with outstanding care and judgement, with a working knowledge of trade English (the *lingua franca* of the Coast) and an immense respect for the traders white and black, in out of the way places who had made her so welcome. 'Only Me' was their nickname for the travel-stained but exquisitely mannered English lady who would appear unheralded on the veranda of the remote bush factory or on the river wharf where they were sorting their goods, observing 'It's only me!' Of this first visit to Africa she has left little account, but certain startling incidents are to be found embedded like plums in the serious pudding of her *West African Studies*. To this early period belongs, for instance, her friendship with the witch doctor who took her out one night for a long, weird walk to a remote village where he had a patient on whom he wanted Miss Kingsley's opinion. This no doubt helped to provide material for the lecture on 'Therapeutics from the point of view of an African witch doctor', which she delivered later to the London Society of Medicine for Women. She learnt in these early days to travel rough, living off the country on unappetizing 'native chop' on which she has many amusing things to say. The manioc meal which was the staple food on all her journeys might be met with under countless names so that 'if ever I meet a tribe that refers to buttered muffins I shall know what to expect and so not get excited'. Often the poisonous element in this ubiquitous root might not be properly soaked out, the fish might be dried and 'properly known as stink-fish', the smoked meat might be burnt and hard; all in all, 'you may understand why on the Coast, when a man comes in and says he has been down on native chop, we say "Good gracious!" and give out the best tins on the spot'.

She learnt too about ships—principally from Captain Murray with whom she sailed from Liverpool, who taught her navigation, how to stow cargo and, no doubt, how to manage a native crew. She inherited from adventurous Kingsley ancestors a passion for the sea, which expressed itself in dreams of heaven on 'the deck of an African liner in the Bights, watching her funnel and masts swinging to and fro against the sky'; it also expressed itself in a ferocious practical talent for all nautical matters—for swarming up a rope ladder, coaxing a tricky engine, steering in a rough sea or in rockstrewn water inshore. When she came to write her book, she took meekly enough suggestions on points of grammar and the like, but be corrected on seamanship she would not. 'I say you can go across Forçados Bar drawing eighteen feet,' she wrote to her publisher, George Macmillan, 'The Dr. says it has eighteen foot of water on it at low water. It has not. You can go—because you can drive through a foot or two of mud . . . I have taken vessels of 2,000 tons across that Bar and up the Forçados creeks as a pilot, three times. I should never get the chance of taking another if I published such rot, and I would rather take a 200-ton vessel up a creek than write any book.'

She did less than justice to herself here, for she was in fact a splendid writer, not appreciated as such in her own time because her racy, colloquial style too much resembled her seventeenth century favourite *Robberies and Murders of the most Notorious Pirates* exactly to suit Victorian tastes. Consecutive narrative was not her strong point, and it is sometimes difficult to disentangle the sequence of events, but when she said 'I have to show you a series of pictures of things and hope you will get from those pictures the impression which is the truth,' she described her method precisely. She called *Travels in West Africa* 'a word swamp of a book', and so it is if we remember that to Mary Kingsley swamps were beautiful, unpredictable and productive of much comic incident.

She embarked on her second voyage, again from Liverpool, in December 1894 accompanying Lady MacDonald whose husband was Governor of the newly formed Oil Rivers Protectorate, and with whom she spent five months at Calabar, busy on research into fish and fetish. She visited Fernando Po and San Thomé with the MacDonalds, and investigated the way of life of the native Bubis and of the immigrant Spaniards and Portuguese. Back in Calabar she indulged to the full an insatiable appetite for water and mud, paddling about in the mangrove swamps of the Oil Rivers beset by flies and crocodiles.

This is a fascinating pursuit. For people who like that sort of thing it is just the sort of thing they like, as the art critic of a provincial town wisely observed anent an impressionist picture recently acquired for the municipal gallery. But it is a pleasure to be indulged in with caution; for one thing you are certain to come across crocodiles . . . In addition to this unpleasantness you are liable—until you realize the danger from experience, or have native advice on this point—to get tide-trapped away in the swamps, the water falling round you when you are away in some deep pool or lagoon and you find you cannot get back to the main river . . . you stop in your lagoon until the tide rises again; most of your attention is directed to dealing with an 'at home' to crocodiles and mangrove flies and with the fearful stench of the slime round you. What little time you have over you will employ in wondering why you came to West Africa, and why, after having reached this point of absurdity, you need have gone and painted the lily and adorned the rose, by being such a colossal ass as to come fooling about in mangrove swamps . . . On one occasion a mighty Silurian, as the *Daily Telegraph* would call him, chose to get his front paws over the stern of my canoe and endeavoured to improve our acquaintance. I had to retire to the bows to keep the balance right, and fetch him a clip on the snout with a paddle when he withdrew, and I paddled into the very middle of the lagoon, hoping the water there was too deep for him or any of his friends to repeat the performance.

While at Calabar she visited the redoubtable missionary Mary Slessor, a strict Presbyterian Christian who nevertheless was so famous and so sympathetic an expert on the beliefs and customs of the tribe among which she lived that Miss Kingsley found in her a completely kindred spirit. She has, unfortunately, left very little description and no coherent account of her adventure in the Oil Rivers, characteristically maintaining that she did not know enough to be entitled to write about her researches there.

In May 1895 she left Calabar bound for the Ogowé river in the French Congo to collect the particular type of freshwater fish in which she was interested. Furnished with trade goods from Hatton and Cookson's store at Libreville, and armed with introductions from their Agent Mr. Hudson to French Mission stations up stream at Kangwé and Talagouga (she gave a qualified approval to the French Evangelicals) she established a base with M. and Mme Jacot at Kangwé near the now famous island of Lembarené. Her voyage up river introduced her to a great forest 'beyond all my expectations of tropical luxuriance and beauty, and it is a thing of another world to the forest of the Upper Calabar, which beautiful as it is, is a sad dowdy to this. There you certainly get a great sense of grimness and vastness; here you have an equal grimness and vastness with the addition of superb colour . . . It is as full of life and beauty and passion as any symphony Beethoven ever wrote: the parts are changing, interweaving, and returning.' This was the forest in which she was soon to become so much at home that her own identity would fall away and she would become a part of the natural scene as her physical and mental eyes became adjusted to her surroundings.

On first entering the great grim twilight regions of the forest you hardly see anything but the vast column-like grey tree stems in their countless thousands around you, and the sparsely vege-tated ground beneath. But day by day, as you get trained to your surroundings, you see more and more, and a whole world grows up gradually out of the gloom before your eyes. Snakes, beetles, bats and beasts, people the region that at first seemed lifeless . . . There is the same difference also between night and day in the forest. You may have got fairly used to it by day, and then some catastrophe keeps you out in it all night, and again you see another world. To my taste there is nothing so fascinating as spending a night out in an African forest, or plantation; but I beg you to note I do not advise any one to follow the practice. Nor indeed do I recommend African forest life to any one. Unless you are interested in it and fall under its charm, it is the most awful life in death imaginable. It is like being shut up in a library whose books you cannot read, all the while tormented, terrified, and bored. And if you do fall under its spell, it takes all the colour out of other kinds of living.

She took off from the French Mission at Talagouga, above Kangwé, for a daring sally over the Ogowé rapids in search of fish:

I establish myself on my portmanteau comfortably in the canoe, my back is against the trade box, and behind that is the usual mound of pillows, sleeping mats, and mosquito-bars of the Igalwa crew; the whole surmounted by the French flag flying from an indifferent stick . . . M. and Mme. Forget provide me with everything I can possibly require, and say, that the blood of half my crew is half alcohol; on the whole it is patent they don't expect to see me again, and I forgive them, because they don't seem cheerful over it; but still it is not reassuring, nothing is about this affair, and it's going to rain. It does, as we go up the river to Njole, where there is another risk of the affair collapsing, by the French authorities declining to allow me to proceed.

However, she would not be deterred and got away from Njole with cries of 'Adieu Mademoiselle' in a 'for-ever tone of voice' ringing in her ears. Above Njole the river narrowed into a swift current and they had to manhandle the canoe round the bends, the men crying at intervals 'Jump for bank, sar! and I "up and jumped", followed by half the crew. One appalling corner I shall not forget, for I had to jump at a rock wall, and hang on to it in a manner more befitting an insect than an insect-hunter, and then scramble up into it into a close-set forest, heavily burdened with boulders of all sizes. I wonder whether the rocks or the trees were there first?' Not even the most imminent peril could paralyse her enquiring mind. They stopped at a village inhabited by the 'brisk and excitable Fans' Mary's favourite tribe, to ask news of the distances and dangers ahead of them. The Chief gave them good advice about the villages up river, laying variously sized leaves at intervals along the edge of the canoe in a primitive kind of map to represent each place and the distances between. The fourth was the only one he could conscientiously recommend as a staging post. Mary gave him some tobacco and 'M'bo sang them a hymn, with the assistance of Pierre, half a line behind him in a different key; but every bit as flat. The Fans seemed impressed, but any crowd would be by the hymn-singing of my crew, unless they were inmates of deaf and dumb asylums.' After an argument with the current just above the village, during which Miss Kingsley 'did my best to amuse the others by diving headlong from a large rock on to which I had elaborately climbed, into a thick clump of willow leaved shrubs', they got well away up stream. The 'Fan mile', however, proved 'a bit Irish' and as the stars came out in a purple velvet sky, they were still scanning the banks in vain for the hospitable village represented by leaf four in the Fan chief's map. Dark fell as they struck a current like a mill race coming through a ravine 'like an alley-way made of iron' and they 'met the rapids in earnest, hissing in whirls of spray round savage rocks' in which they finally jammed, only to be swept back down stream. Cast up eventually on an island, they left the canoe wedged among rocks and struggled through a patch of forest strewn with boulders towards a far-away light and the 'good old rump-a-tump-tump-tump tune of a drum'—a sound which Mary claimed called up the Neolithic man in her. She made friends at once with the crowd of vermillion-painted dancers and, taking possession of the village club-house, sat serenely awaiting her dinner which she ate while the devout M'bo conducted a religious service in the street outside. Afterwards, while the men settled to their meal, she wandered off into the night to the bank of the 'foaming, flying Ogowé in its deep ravine'.

> In the darkness round me flitted thousands of fireflies and out beyond this pool of utter night flew by unceasingly the white foam of the rapids; sound there was none save their thunder. The majesty and beauty of the scene fascinated me, and I stood leaning with my back against a rock pinnacle watching it. Do not imagine it gave rise, in what I am pleased to call my mind, to those complicated, poetical reflections natural beauty seems to bring out in other people's minds. It never works that way with me; I just lose all sense of human individuality, all memory of human life, with its grief and worry and doubt, and become part of the atmosphere. If I have a heaven that will be mine.

Next morning saw them on their way up stream again over the rapids, and eventually they reached a high enough point for Mary to collect the fish she wanted, selecting them and pickling them with her usual meticulous care. She returned from Talagouga on the official launch, passing the time by stitching a new braid round the hem of her skirt (it had become rather bedraggled in the fight with the rapids) and in savouring the natural beauties of the scene. Her enjoyment of the human vagaries of shipboard life was diminished, though by no means extinguished, by her complete ignorance of the French language. Back at the Mission she set herself to perfect her skill in paddling a canoe, an art she had acquired while at Talagouga. 'Success crowned my efforts' she declared 'and I can honestly say that there are only two things I am proud of—one is that Doctor Gunther has approved of my fishes, and the other is that I can paddle an Ogowé canoe. Pace, style, steering and all "All same for one" as if I were an Ogowé African.' Once she could do this, there was no keeping her quiet and she was constantly on the move, paddling over to Lembarené, or up the Ogowé with her goods to visit the villages on the banks and beyond in the bush. Once she fell down a steep hillside through the roof of a Fan hut and had to pay the master of the house for the damage to his roof and the shock to the nerves of his old mother by a draft on Hatton and Cookson.

She was restless, however, to go further afield. Fish there

might be in the neighbourhood of the Mission, but for what she was apt to call 'good, rank fetish' she must get away from European influence. North of the Ogowé lay a belt of forest inhabited by Fans related to those Mary had come to know on her journeys up stream, but in an altogether wilder state. The Fans were a primitive and virile people from the interior who were driving their way through the bush towards the coast lands, ousting the more civilized tribes who had come within the missionary sphere and who had learnt to trade with the white man, to wear clothes and to furnish their houses with something more cosy than weapons and charms. The Fans were known to eat human flesh, not as some tribes did in religious ritual, but as a staple article of diet. Mary had taken a great fancy to those she had met; she admired their 'fire, temper, intelligence and go', and was quite undisturbed by their evil reputation as dangerous cannibals. She held it to be 'no danger, I think, to white people except as to the bother it gives one in preventing one's black companions from being eaten'. She thought it rather fussy of the mission-educated Ajumba to refuse all meat in Fan villages.

In order to see something of this delightful tribe in its natural habitat, Mary aimed to find a way through the forest northward to the Rembwé river on which Hatton and Cookson had one of their bush factories. Here she could pay off her men in trade goods and come down the Rembwé back to Libreville on the Gaboon estuary. Neither her French nor her African friends were very encouraging, in fact the authorities refused to take responsibility for her or to allow her to carry the symbolic protection of the French flag as she had done on the trip up the rapids. There were rumours of war in the bush, and none of the local people knew the way. However, some of the Ajumba claimed to have a trading acquaintance with the Fans who lived a day's canoe-ride away at M'fetta on an island in lake Ncovi who were said to trade with the Rembwé and might be persuaded to provide guides. They were willing to try, and on 22 July 1895 she set off with four men in a canoe, in pouring rain and with a splitting headache. Her crew seemed 'kind and pleasant companions' and she nicknamed them Gray Shirt, Singlet, Silence and Pagan; she also had an Igalwa interpreter, Ngouta, so nervous and ineffective as to be the butt of the whole party, with his 'valueless vocabulary' of 'Praps', ''Tis better so' and 'Lordy, Lordy, helpee me!' Fortunately they could converse in trade English, a kind of pidgin in which Mary was something of an expert.

They spent the first night at the Ajumba village of Arevooma where Gray Shirt placed at Mary's disposal his very superior house furnished with chairs and looking glasses, and with calico sheets on the comfortable bed. A 'slightly awful' prayer meeting made her headache rather worse, but she woke at dawn next morning completely recovered and ready for the long day's canoeing ahead. They were joined by an Ajumba whom she called 'Passenger' who was hoping to find work at John Holt's Rembwé factory. The men were all well armed with guns fully loaded, their flintlocks sheathed in gorilla or leopard skin. They glided down the main stream through flocks of lovely birds, greeted by passing canoes loaded with fruit and punted by singing Africans: a 'most luxuriant, charming and pleasant trip.' Presently they turned north into an unmapped river and after drawing on to a sandbank for Miss Kingsley's tea and a pipe for the men, they paddled on into a 'strange, wild, lonely bit of the world', and one of the men remarked 'All Fan now' in 'anything but a gratified tone of voice.' As they passed an island, her observant mind noted that 'the grass is stubbled down into paths by hippos and just as I have realized who are the road-makers, they appear in person. One immense fellow, hearing us, stands up and shows himself about six feet from us in the grass, gazes calmly, and then yawns a yawn a yard wide and grunts his news to his companions, some of whom—there is evidently a large herd—get up and stroll towards us with all the flowing grace of Pantechnicon vans in motion.' Were they, she wondered, the first or last of creatures? Had Nature's prentice hand perpetrated them, or had she tired of all her beautiful creations and exclaimed at last: 'Here, just put these other viscera into big bags—I can't bother any more.' Avoiding the hippos, they ran into crocodiles, and the scene took on a striking resemblance to the pictures of intrepid explorers in the story-books of her childhood.

They came out of the winding river into Lake Ncovi towards evening, a sinister, silent stretch of water rising in luminous silver bubbles as the paddles struck the surface. 'Singlet' exclaiming that he smelt blood, voiced the party's uneasiness and as they drove the canoe boldly on the rocks of a large island, a mass of Africans poured down the hillside, fingering their guns and loosening their long knives; these were the men of M'fetta among whom 'Pagan' hoped to recognize a friend. 'Silence' spoke up for once, observing:

'It would be bad palaver if Kiva no live for this place'. I got up from my seat . . . and leisurely strolled ashore, saying to the line of angry faces 'M'boloani' in an unconcerned way, although I well knew it was etiquette for them to salute first. They grunted, but did not commit themselves further. A minute after they parted to allow a fine-looking, middle-aged man, naked save for a twist of dirty cloth round his loins and a bunch of leopard and wild cat tails hung from his shoulder by a strip of leopard skin, to come forward. Pagan went for him with a rush, as if he were going to clasp him to his ample bosom, but holding his hand just off from touching the Fan's shoulder in the usual way, while he said in Fan, 'Don't you know me, my beloved Kiva? Surely you have not forgotten your old friend?' Kiva grunted feelingly, and raised up his hands and held them just off touching Pagan, and we breathed again. Then Gray Shirt made a rush at the crowd and went through great demonstrations of affection with another gentleman whom he recognized as being a Fan friend of his own, and whom he had not expected to meet here. I looked round to see if there was not any Fan from the Upper Ogowé whom I knew to go for, but could not see one that I could on the strength of a previous acquaintance, and on their individual merits I did not feel inclined to do even this fashionable imitation embrace. Indeed I must say that never—even in a picture book—have I seen such a set of wild wicked-looking savages as those we faced this night, and with whom it was touch-and-go for twenty of the longest minutes I have ever lived.

The natives, however, decided not to be hostile, and the party was welcomed, Mary walking boldly through the crowd which fell back in amazement at her strange appearance, at her long black skirt, high-necked blouse, cummerbund and closely-fitting hat; the children howled at the sight of her white face. Housed in a hut which, though remarkably filthy, with a rough wooden bench for a bed, was the best in the town, Mary called for her tea, and invited the village to provide carriers to come with her to the Rembwé. Some hours of stormy palaver resulted in the engagement of four bold, buccaneering spirits who delighted Miss Kingsley and frightened her men into fits. Kiva and Wiki were famous hunters and skilled in bushcraft, Fika was 'a fine young fellow' and the fourth member of the party, 'a Fan gentleman with the manners of a duke and the habits of a dustbin', came uninvited and unpaid 'to see the fun, and drop in for a fight if there was one going on'. From the first, Mary made friends with the Fans, making about them that curious remark I have already quoted.

We each recognized we belonged to that same section of the human race with whom it is better to drink than to fight. We knew we would each have killed the other, if sufficient inducement were offered, and so we took a certain amount of care that the inducement should not arise. Gray Shirt and Pagan also, their trade friends, the Fans treated with an independent sort of courtesy; but Silence, Singlet, the Passenger, and above all Ngouta, they openly did not care a row of pins for, and I have small doubt that had it not been for us other three they would have killed and eaten those amiable gentlemen with as much compunction as an English sportsman would kill as many rabbits. They on their part hated the Fan and never lost an opportunity of telling me 'These Fan be bad man too much'.

The way to the Rembwé lay through a dense forest of ebony and hardwood trees, rising to 100 or even 150 feet high, their tangled branches making a canopy to shut out the sun, hung with creepers and vines, or bush-ropes, which reminded the nautical Miss Kingsley of ships' rigging. The first day's march was a long one, twenty-five miles from the point where they disembarked from their canoe, up to the knees in black slime. The Fans set a spanking pace, leaving the Ajumba, fine canoe men but no walkers, panting behind and only able to keep up because the Fans had to stop every two hours to stoke their enormous appetites. Mary strode along somewhere between the two groups, and was rewarded when ahead of both by the sight of five great elephants enjoying a mud bath in the hollow into which their path was falling. She was joined by Kiva to whom she suggested an elephant hunt, but he shook his head sadly; their party was not strong enough and anyway they would need all their ammunition for the hostile Fans they were sure to meet. As they began to climb into the foot-hills of the Sierra del Cristal they had to clamber over great falls of rotting timber, cluttering the slopes to depths of twenty feet or more, into which, one after another, they fell crashing through among 'more snakes and centipedes . . . than you had any immediate use for, even though you were a collector; but there you had to stay while Wiki, who was a most critical connoisseur, selected from the surrounding forest a bush-rope that he regarded as the correct remedy for your case, and then up you were hauled, through the sticks you had turned the wrong way on your down journey'. Very inadequate, Wiki told them, was the bush-rope they used to pull him up when his turn came; the thought of this occasion 'makes the perspiration run down my nose whenever I think of it'. The stretches of forest between these hazards was incredibly beautiful, but there was no time to linger if they were to reach Efoua that night, a town where the Fans were pretty sure they had friends, but did not want to risk breaking into after dark in case they had not. By five o'clock they were nearing the town and:

The path was slightly indistinct, but by keeping my eye on it I could see it. Presently I came to a place where it went out, but appeared again the other side of a clump of underbush fairly distinctly. I made a short cut for it and the next news was I was in a heap, on a lot of spikes, some fifteen feet or so below ground level, at the bottom of a bag-shaped game pit.

It is at these times you realize the blessing of a good thick skirt. Had I paid heed to the advice of many people in England, who ought to have known better, and did not do it themselves, and adopted masculine garments, I should have been spiked to the bone and done for. Whereas, save for a good many bruises here was I with the fulness of my skirt tucked under me, sitting on nine ebony spikes some twelve inches long, in comparative comfort, howling lustily to be hauled out. The Duke came along first, and looked down at me. I said, 'Get a bush-rope and haul me out.' He grunted and sat down on a log. The Passenger came next, and he looked down, 'You kill?' says he. 'Not much,' say I; 'Get a bush-rope and haul me out.' 'No fit' says he, and sat down on the log. Presently, however, Kiva and Wiki came up, and Wiki went and selected the one and only bush-rope suitable to haul an English lady, of my exact complexion, age, and size, out of that one particular pit. They seemed rare round there from the time he took; and I was just casting about in my mind as to what method would be best to employ in getting up the smooth, yellow, sandy-clay incurved walls, when he arrived with it, and I was out in a twinkling, and very much ashamed of myself until Silence, who was then leading, disappeared through the path before us with a despairing yell. Each man then pulled the skin cover off his gun lock, carefully looked to see if things were all right and ready loosened his knife in its snake-skin sheath; and then we set about hauling poor Silence out, binding him up where necessary with cool green leaves; for he, not having a skirt, had got a good deal frayed at the edges on those spikes.

At Efoua they were again regarded with much surprise, but luckily no hostility; until, that is, the Duke was set upon by the townspeople who accused him of the murder of one of their number in the not too distant past. They weathered this, however, for lack of evidence, and Mary spent a not very restful night curled up among her boxes with a sack of tobacco for a pillow. Awaking to a strange smell, she located some grisly human remains hanging in a bag overhead; calmly tipping into her hat ('for fear of losing anything of value') a shrivelled hand, some toes, eyes and ears, she registered in her notebook the Fan custom of 'keeping mementoes of their victims'. Was this hat the moleskin pillbox which is the pride of the Royal Geographical Society's Museum?

Their next stop was Egaja, a town of evil reputation where none of them had any acquaintance. They had an exhausting march up and down hill with constant falls through the layers of rotten timber on the slopes, and in and out of a succession of swamps in the ravines. They took it in turns to lead, Mary with the rest, finding by trial and error the fords through the 'black batter-like ooze' or over the thin, sun-baked crust of the swamps. There was trouble brewing among the escort. The Fans 'were in high feather, openly insolent to Ngouta, and anxious for me to stay in this delightful locality, and go hunting with them and divers other choice spirits, whom they assured me we could easily get to join as at Efoua'. Mary, however, kept the peace, and talked her way into Egaja by briskly telling the chief she had heard his was a 'thief town' and she trusted him to prove the contrary. She not only talked cleverly; she proved her goodwill by doctoring the chief's mother who had such a disgusting abscess on her arm that even the strong-stomached Miss Kingsley was nearly sick on the spot and took the precaution of having her tea before getting down to serious surgery. They did not get out of Egaja without a row, Kiva being challenged for payment of an old debt. They had him tied up in no time, and Miss Kingsley settled down to a long, instructive and highly enjoyable 'law palaver' (had she not come to Africa to study the customs of the natives?) in the course of which she played a considerable part herself, taking the floor with the ceremonial 'Azuna!'—'Silence, I am speaking!' She bought off Kiva with some of her trade goods, and decided to get out of Egaja before Wiki, 'who was pleading an alibi and a twin brother, in a bad wife palaver' stirred up any more trouble.

It was on the third day's march that Wiki showed her the gorillas—five of them:

> One old male, one young male, and three females. One of these had clinging to her a young fellow with beautiful wavy black hair with just a kink in it. The big male was crouching on his haunches, with his long arms hanging down on either side, with the backs of his hands on the ground, the palms upwards. The elder lady was tearing to pieces and eating a pine-apple, while the others were at the plantains destroying more than they ate . . . I put out my hand and laid it on Wiki's gun to prevent him from firing, and he, thinking I was going to fire, gripped my wrist. I watched the gorillas with great interest for a few seconds, until I heard Wiki make a peculiar small sound, and looking at him saw his face was working in an awful way as he clutched his throat with his hand violently. Heavens! think I, this gentleman's going to have a fit; it's lost we are entirely this time. He rolled his head to and fro, and then buried his face into a heap of dried rubbish at the foot of a plantain stem, clasped his hands over it, and gave an explosive sneeze. The gorillas let go all, raised themselves up for a second, gave a quaint sound between a bark and a howl, and then the ladies and the young gentleman started for home.

Presently they crossed a river flowing north-west in the hoped-for direction of the Rembwé. They began to meet, too, bands of local rubber collectors, and Wiki and Kiva gave her a lesson in trade practices, telling her how the rubber was first milked from the rubber vines, then boiled down by the women in the villages and rolled into balls which there were many ingenious ways of doctoring to make them appear larger. These and the ivory from the men's hunting parties were sold to itinerant African traders, or to the nearest bush factory, from where they were carried through the hands of several middlemen to the white traders of the coast towns. All information was grist to her mill; everything built up her picture of an untamed country, where danger simmered just below the surface, adding zest to her travels, a flavour to the endless cups of tea which were her one indulgence. Everything went down in her notebook, though she confesses to failure in following the advice of 'a valued scientific friend'—'Always take measurements, Miss Kingsley, and always take them from the adult male.'

The rubber collectors, and patches of cultivated ground, heralded Esoon, a comparatively quiet town which:

> Endeared itself to me by knowing the Rembwé, and not just waving the arm in the air, in any direction, and saying 'Far far plenty bad people live for that side' as other towns had done. Of course they stuck to the bad people part of the legend; but I was getting quite callous as to the moral character of new acquaintances, feeling sure that for good solid murderous rascality several of my old Fan acquaintances, and even my own party would take quite a lot of beating.

All the same, she felt obliged to take account of the 'blood war' blocking the direct path to the Rembwé. The next village was shooting strangers on sight, and had rigged up a signal system of trip wires and bells at the approaches.

> The Duke, who as I have said before, was a fine courageous fellow, ready to engage in any undertaking, suggested I should go up the road—alone by myself—first—a mile ahead of the party— and the next town, perhaps, might not shoot at sight, if they happened to notice I was something queer; and I might explain things, and then the rest of the party would follow. 'There's nothing like dash and courage, my dear Duke,' I said, 'even if one displays it by deputy, so this plan of yours does you great credit; but as my knowledge of this charming language of yours is but small, I fear I might create a wrong impression in that town, and it might think I had kindly brought them a present of eight edible heathens—you and the remainder of my followers,

you understand.' My men saw this was a real danger, and this was the only way I saw of excusing myself. It is at such moments as this that the Giant's robe gets, so to speak, between your legs and threatens to trip you up. Going up a forbidden road, and exposing yourself as a pot shot to ambushed natives would be jam and fritters to Mr. MacTaggart, for example; but I am not up to that form yet.

She persuaded them to the alternative of a detour, to strike the Rembwé at N'dorko down stream from Agonjo where she believed the trading posts of both Hatton and Cookson and John Holt to be and, resuming the boots she had taken off for the first time since leaving the Ogowé, she led her men smartly off by a path going west-north-west from Esoon. This landed them in a mangrove swamp which she observed only just in time was tidal, a long arm of the sea from the Gaboon estuary. And the tide was clearly on the make. They had to turn and run for it and for over an hour they scrambled through liquid mud and 'solid stench' in the tropical afternoon sun until they reached a safe, dry hillside. Here they struck a path running east over a stream cascading prettily to the north and the Rembwé and came to plantations in the late afternoon. Beyond the planted ground lay a valley, Turneresque in its misty beauty, but containing a swamp in which a woman was wading through up to her armpits. Out of this bog with no more than a wetting, they fell in with a party of men and women carrying rubber to N'dorko, now quite close and said to be just beyond the next swamp.

It stretched away in all directions, a great sheet of filthy water, out of which sprang gorgeous marsh plants, in islands, great banks of screw pine, and coppices of wine palm, with their lovely fronds reflected back by the still mirror-like water, so that the reflection was as vivid as the reality . . . Our path went straight into this swamp over the black rocks forming its rim, in an imperative, no alternative 'Come-straight-along-this-way' style. Singlet, who was leading, carrying a good load of bottled fish and a gorilla specimen, went at it like a man, and disappeared before the eyes of us close following him, then and there down through the water . . . I said we must get the rubber carriers who were coming this way to show us the ford; and so we sat down on the bank, a tired, disconsolate, dilapidated-looking row, until they arrived. When they came up they did not plunge in forthwith; but leisurely set about making a most nerve-shaking set of preparations, taking off their clothes, and forming them into bundles, which, to my horror, they put on the tops of their heads. The men went in first, each holding his gun high above his head. They skirted the bank before they struck out into the swamp and were followed by the women and by our party, and soon we were all up to our chins.

We were two hours and a quarter passing that swamp; I was one hour and three-quarters; but I made good weather of it, closely following the rubber-carriers, and only going in right over head and all twice. Other members of my band were less fortunate. One finding himself getting out of his depth, got hold of a palm frond and pulled himself into deeper water still, and had to roost among the palms until a special expedition of the tallest men went and gathered him like a flower. Another got himself mixed up and scratched because he thought to make a short cut through screw pines. He did not know the screw pine's little ways, and he had to have a special relief expedition. One and all, we got horribly infested with leeches, having a frill of them round our necks like astrakhan collars, and our hands covered with them when we came out. The depth of the swamp is very uniform, at its ford we went in up to our necks, and climbed up on to the rocks on the hither side out of water equally deep.

They staggered at last into N'dorko on the banks of the Rembwé caked in mud, devoured by leeches and beset with flies. Here she was met by a civil-spoken African who was Hatton and Cookson's sub-agent, and accosted rather than met by a representative of the rival firm of John Holt who looked 'generally as if he had come out of a pantomime on the *Arabian Nights*' and 'dashed through the crowd, shouting "I'm for Holty! I'm for Holty"!' She bought tobacco and cloth from one and rum from the other, later paddling up stream to Agonjo where Hatton and Cookson's main factory was situated and where she was able to rest for a few days. She paid off her men in goods, and came down the river in spanking style with an African trader called Obanjo—'but he liked it pronounced Captain Johnson'. 'There was a Hallo-my-Hearty atmosphere coming off him from the top of his hat to the soles of his feet like the scent of a flower,' and Mary summed him up as one of the five men of her acquaintance whom she could have trusted as a bush companion—'one of us at least would have come out alive and have made something substantial by the venture'.

Mary Kingsley, 1862–1900

'He wore, when first we met, a huge sombrero hat, a spotless singlet, and a suit of clean, well-got-up-dungarees, and an uncommonly picturesque, powerful figure he cut in them with his finely-moulded, well-knit form and good-looking face, full of expression always, but always with the keen small eyes in it watching the effect his genial smiles and hearty laugh produced. The eyes were the eyes of Obanjo, the rest of the face the property of Captain Johnson.' She made 'the slowest white man time on record' down the Rembwé, partly owing to the half-finished state of Captain Johnson's canoe, and the dilapidated bed-quilt which served as a sail, partly owing to the extensive and complicated trade affairs which had to be dealt with, and the local feuds which had to be side-stepped. She offered to take over the tiller at night, and when the captain realized she knew what she was about, he handed over the ship every evening.

> Much as I have enjoyed life in Africa, I do not think I ever enjoyed it to the full as I did on those nights dropping down the Rembwé. The great, black, winding river with a pathway in its midst of frosted silver where the moonlight struck it; on each side the ink-black mangrove walls, and above them the band of star and moonlit heavens that the walls of mangrove allowed one to see. Forward rose the form of our sail, idealized from bed-sheetdom to glory; and the little red glow of our cooking fire gave a single note of warm colour to the cold light of the moon.

Celebrating her return to civilization at the estuary mouth by rolling off the deck in her sleep into the harbour water, it was something of an anti-climax to land and be met by Mr. Hudson: 'I was nervous about meeting him, knowing that since he had carefully deposited me in safe hands with Mme. Jacot, with many injunctions to be careful, that there were many incidents in my career that would not meet with his approval . . . He did not approve. He had heard of most of my goings on.'

An opportunity now offered of combining fish and fetish by visiting the island of Corisco where she was told the women fished the inland lakes in a special way at special seasons. The island was a day's sail across Corisco Bay, and was reached pleasantly enough in the *Lafayette*, 'a fine, seaworthy boat' lent her by Dr. Nassau, a seasoned and scholarly missionary from whom Mary learnt much about the tribes of the interior, such as the Fan, and the more easy-going, and to her far less interest-

169

ing and admirable, people of the coast. Corisco was a disappointment, the people were lethargic and altogether too good-natured, there was nothing very interesting after all about the fishing customs, and the fish were commonplace. She was soon on board the *Lafayette* again, stowing the cargo to her liking and settling in the passengers who had turned up uninvited for a lift to the mainland. 'I find I am expected to sit surrounded by a rim of alligator pears and bananas, as though I were some kind of joint garnished for table, instead of a West Coast skipper,' but she soon took the helm, steering the *Lafayette* through high seas until with the approach of evening the wind dropped, and they were becalmed. Anchoring on a spit of sand after 'energetically taking soundings over the stern with my umbrella'—'it is magnificent, but not navigation, still it works well'—they camped on board for the night. The crew made a tent of the mainsail under which they huddled out of reach of the dangerous moonlight with 'a large ram Mr. Ibea is sending to Gaboon, and that sheep has scimitar-shaped sharp horns and restless habits, and I can see he does things that hurt and rouse the sleepers to groaning-point perpetually'. As for Mary, the ridiculous blended as usual with the sublime as she sat in the stern gazing at the:

Motionless black line of forest with the soft white mist rolling low and creeping and crawling out between its stems from the lagoons behind the sand-ridged beach. The mist comes stretching out from under the bushes over the sand towards the sea, now raising itself up into peaks, now crouching down upon the sand, and sending out long white arms or feelers towards the surf and then drawing them back as if it were some spirit-possessed thing, poisonous and malignant, that wanted to reach us, and yet is timorous and frightened of the surf's thunder-roar and spray . . . I don't think this sort of mist is healthy, but it is often supremely lovely and always fascinates me . . . I have, when benighted, walked hurriedly through it for miles in the forest while it has mischievously hidden the path at my feet from the helpful illumination of the moon, swishing and swirling round my moving skirts . . . I have often, when no one has been near to form opinions of my frivolity, played with it, scooping it up in my hands and letting it fall again, or swished it about with a branch, when it lay at a decent level or three or four feet from the ground.

Jerked out of her dream by the dragging of the *Lafayette*'s anchor and the nerve-shattering snores of the crew, crouched under their improvised tent for all the world like corpses draped in a grave-cloth, the rougher side of her nature asserted itself. Having secured the ship, she layed about the crew with a stout branch of plantains, not much minding who was disturbed so long as the snores were silenced.

She was glad on the whole to arrive at Hatton and Cookson's wharf, and after a short rest she embarked on a homeward bound steamer calling at Cameroon river in German territory. Mary had an admiration for Germany and the Germans founded partly on the idea, once popular with our grandparents but out of fashion today, that there was a racial affinity between Briton and Teuton; partly, no doubt, on her proficiency in their language. Comparisons would be interesting, she suggested, between the English, French, German, Portuguese and Spanish administrations in Africa, but it was not the idea of making such a survey that kept her in the Cameroons: it was a whim which had grown to a passion to ascend the Cameroon Mountain, Mungo Mah Lobeh—the Throne of Thunder. She admits that climbing mountains had no place in her programme, there being no fish on them and few people to practise fetish, but ever since her first sight of the two peaks of the Big and Little Cameroon, as she sailed along the coast in 1893, she had longed to stand on this highest point of West Africa.

She chose the difficult south-east, or landward, side for her attempt and was only the second climber to reach the top. She tells the story in her usual rollicking fashion—there were mishaps, raptures, triumphs and comic disasters enough, but through it all runs a sense of strain not apparent in her far more dangerous adventures on the Ogowé. The carriers and servants she took with her were feckless and faint-hearted and she missed her Fan friends; she was not amused by the local people who crowded into the Mission hut where she took shelter for the night; when she reached the summit it was so swathed in mist that she could see no more than a few feet in front of her. She was, one senses, coming dangerously near that point reached by so many great travellers when danger and hardship cease to be a challenge and become an addiction, when the leader begins to chivy instead of to encourage. Livingstone driving his Makololo friends across the burning stones of the Kebrabasa gorge; Joseph Thomson, ill and spent himself, yet showing no mercy on his smallpox-ridden caravan; Isabella Bird struggling through the blizzard on the further confines of China; Marianne North, deaf, frightened, exhausted yet determined to paint one more tree before she gave up—Mary Kingsley had not yet reached such a point of no return, but the Cameroon ascent shows her near it. And how it rained! Water, drenching from the skies, barring her path, saturating her skirts, is the leit-motif of the journey and provides, incidentally a very curious instance of the way Victorian inhibitions could reassert themselves. 'I am in an awful mess', she writes, describing the fording of a river.

> Mud-caked skirts, and blood-stained hands and face. Shall I make an exhibition of myself by going unwashed to that unknown German officer who is in charge of the station? Naturally I wash here, standing in the river and swishing the mud out of my skirts, but what is life without a towel . . . I receive a most kindly welcome from a fair, grey-eyed German gentleman, only unfortunately I see my efforts to appear before him clean and tidy have been quite unavailing, for he views my appearance with unmixed horror, and suggests an instant hot bath. I decline. Men can be trying! How in the world is anyone going to take a bath in a house with no doors, and only very sketchy window-shutters?

It is on record that in London decorum prevented her riding in a bus, and that she heartily disapproved of that chariot of the Victorian 'New Woman', the bicycle. She was also, incidentally, warmly opposed to women's suffrage.

She landed at Liverpool on 30 November 1895, to be greeted by newspaper correspondents and to find herself a celebrity. Her fame grew with the publication a year later, by Macmillan's, of *Travels in West Africa*, a splendid book, as has already been said, but still not telling half her story. When boiled down to mere facts, the *Travels* describes one journey by water over the Ogowé rapids, one by land through the bush to the Rembwé, neither lasting more than a week; a random selection of excursions, by canoe and on foot, within range of European settlements in Gaboon and Calabar; a sea trip to Corisco; and the ascent of Mungo Mah Lobeh. But there were many more adventures, some of which have been rescued from oblivion by her biographers, out of letters to friends, from lectures printed in obscure school magazines, even from conversations. Some of them she purposely omitted from her *Travels*, out of modesty perhaps, or a fear of not being believed —the whole of an expedition, it would seem, into the Ouronogou country north of the Ogowé, where she helped a village to kill a man-eating crocodile and, finding herself incommoded by a hippopotamus on a small island, urged the creature to leave by tickling it with her umbrella. She told the Cheltenham girls of how she traded her blouses to a party of naked Fans; she told the Eton boys of how a lucky shot from a Fan gun saved her from a gorilla on the way to Rembwé—which explains how 'Singlet' came by the gorilla specimen which was lost in the great swamp near N'dorko. As for the story of the Bishop and the Governor fighting on the cabin floor of the Ogowé launch, she was persuaded by friends to delete this from her book as being too frivolous. And only by chance was the most extraordinary story of all recorded—of how she let out of a trap a magnificent leopard which was beating itself to death against the bars. When it stood for a moment before her, free and bewildered, she stamped her foot at it and said 'Go home, you fool!' and the leopard turned away into the bush. Was she never frightened her friends asked her? It seemed not, though there had been some very tight corners when she had felt 'a strong salt taste' in her mouth, and known she must take things very seriously to survive.

She meant of course to go back to Africa as soon as her book was finished and as soon as she could be spared by her brother, a younger and less effective Charles Kingsley who did a bit of desultory travelling himself, and for whom she kept house whenever he needed her. But not only domestic duties held her, year after year. She became plunged in controversy, as she was bound to be. An enthusiast to whom all experience was significant, she had formed opinions during her two visits to West Africa which she knew to be well founded and felt with all her soul to be important. It was equally inevitable that she should meet with disagreement, for these opinions were unorthodox. The Negro was not a lawless savage; he lived by precise and binding rules which the white man disturbed at his peril. The traders were not a set of dissolute ruffians debauching the natives with imported gin; the African had enjoyed his glass long before the merchants came, and gin was probably better for him than home-brewed palm wine. Most unwelcome of all was her contention that on the whole the missionaries did more harm than good in destroying the restraints along with the licence of the African's ancient religion and offering instead the imperfectly understood Christianity which so few Europeans practised in all its implications. She did not dispute Britain's right to govern Africa, but she warmly disputed Britain's method of doing so, fighting to the last the imposition of European law and religion on peoples with ancient and intricate laws and religions of their own. This imposition was part and parcel of her *bête noire*, the Crown Colony system, administered in a remote and half-hearted spirit from Whitehall and taking no account of the views of the men on the spot. The taxing of a man's own property, for instance, was totally alien to the African idea of equity, and by imposing the hut tax in the Sierra Leone Protectorate in 1896 the British Government had put themselves disastrously in the wrong. Typically, she wasted no time in indictments of the Government for the brutality with which the tax was being collected and the resulting disorders in Sierra Leone repressed; she kept her powder and shot not for the local police and tax-gatherers but for a Government so ignorant that it could violate the African's idea of the sacredness of property by putting a tax on his house. She based her opposition to the hut tax on her considerable knowledge, practical as well as theoretical, of African law as she had studied it on the West Coast, and in August 1897 she addressed the British Association on the subject. In 1897 she published *West African Studies* which contains the results of her research, and sets forth at length her theories on how West Africa should be administered. Why would not those in authority join her in what was the aim of all her adventures—'trying to understand things?' 'All that is wanted is proper method', she insisted, 'And this method I assure you that Science, true knowledge, that which Spinoza termed the inward aid of God, can give you. I am not Science, but only one of her brick-makers, and I beg you to turn to her. Remember you have tried to do without her in African matters for 400 years, and on the road to civilization and advance there you have travelled on a cabbage leaf.' Invited by the great Joseph Chamberlain, Colonial Secretary since 1895, to make positive suggestions, she worked out a system under which the traders should have the chief responsibility for administering West African territories. For the trader knew the African as no one else could know him; the Chambers of Commerce in Liverpool and Manchester and other great cities should be the seat of power, not Whitehall. Side by side with areas administered by the traders, the African should be encouraged to administer his own territory by his own laws, purged by British influence from such abuses as human sacrifice and slave trading. Trade was, or should be, England's only respectable reason for being in Africa at all. She had little patience with the philanthropists who contended that Europe was staking a claim in Africa for the good of the native population. Look what had come out of King Leopold's International African Association, with its high-sounding aims—the Congo Free State, a scandalous instance of white interference in Africa for the wrong reasons. Though she was not in sympathy with the evangelizing of Africa, she could respect the 'true missionary' who might be imagined as thinking it a duty to kill a man to save his soul—the philanthropist who could kill a man's soul to save his life was a being not to be endured.

Her amazing exploits, her vigorous expression of novel opinions and her important connections in both the social and academic worlds brought her enough attention to have turned a head less firmly in place than Mary's. Her advice was sought in high places and the columns of the country's leading newspapers were open to her; the British Museum welcomed her fishes and called three of them after her; she was sought after as a lecturer and loved as a friend; her books were best-sellers. She had an extraordinary faculty for keeping on good terms even with those whose views she opposed, putting her finger casually on a rare quality in her nature when she observed in one of her charming asides 'It is merely that I have the power of bringing out in my fellow-creatures, white or black, their virtues, in a way honourable to them and fortunate for me.' It is only possible to believe her own assurance that she had never been in love and that no one had ever been in love with her when one recollects the intensity of her emotional response to nature and to the wild solitudes of Africa. For what is love if not the complete emotional surrender of the individual, if not to another individual, then to religion, or, as with some of the great poets, to the impersonal grandeur of the sky, the forest and the sea? 'My people are the mangroves, swamps, rivers and the sea, and so on' she wrote once to a friend, 'They never give me the dazzles with their goings-on, like human beings do.' She longed to return to the home where her heart was, to Africa.

She had her eye on remote river country near Lade Chad, but when her chance came at last it was hardly in the way nor to the place she would have chosen. Duty called her to volunteer for nursing service in the South African War, then going badly for the English. She had half an idea of finding some more fishes for Dr. Gunther in the Orange river, but when she arrived it was clear there was to be no time for 'sky-larking'. She asked simply to be sent wherever she could be most useful, where the need was greatest, and was taken at her word with a vengeance. She was sent to nurse Boer prisoners at Simonstown where conditions seem to have been rather reminiscent of Scutari, with the difference that there was 'an unlimited supply of brandy, milk, eggs, champagne, and so on', but with only one doctor and two nurses to cope with an epidemic of enteric fever and measles. 'I never struck such a rocky bit of the valley of the Shadow of Death in all my days' she observed, working night and day and yet finding time for her usual cool and apt observations—'We English are born Imperialists, these men are born nationalists; but I will say no more on that now; it is a rocky problem for the future.' She stood it for two months, helping in her usual quiet and practical way to bring some order into the chaos, and then went down herself with enteric fever, dying after an operation at the age of thirty-eight. By her own last wish she was buried at sea, a voyager to the end.

Bibliography

Bishop, Isabella Bird, *Six Months in the Sandwich Islands*, 1875.
—— *A Lady's Life in the Rocky Mountains*, 1879.
—— *Unbeaten Tracks in Japan*, 1880.
—— *The Golden Chersonese*, 1883.
—— *Journeys in Persia and Kurdistan*, 1891.
—— *Korea and her Neighbours*, 1898.
—— *The Yangtze Valley and Beyond*, 1899.
—— see also, Stoddart, A.
Carey, William, *see* Taylor, Annie R.
Clark, Ronald, *The Victorian Mountaineers*, Batsford, 1953.
Crone, G. R., *The Explorers*, Cassells, 1962.
Davidson, Lilian Campbell, *Hints to Lady Travellers*, 1889.
Duncan, Jane E., *A Summer Ride in Western Tibet*, 1906.
Fleming, Peter, *News from Tartary*, Jonathan Cape, 1938.
—— *Bayonets to Lhasa*, Rupert Hart-Davis, 1955.
Greaves, Rose Louise, *Persia and the Defence of India 1884–1892*, The
    Athlone Press, 1959.
Gwynn, Stephen, *Life of Mary Kingsley*, Macmillan, 1932.
Hore, Annie, *To Lake Tanganyika in a Bath-chair*, 1886.
Howard, Cecil, *Mary Kingsley*, Hutchinson, 1957.
Johnson, Henry, *The Life of Kate Marsden*, 2nd ed., 1895.
Kingsley, Mary, *Travels in West Africa*, 1897.
—— *West African Studies*, 1899.
—— see also, Gwynn, S.; Howard, C.; Wallace, K.
Larymore, Constance, *A Resident's Wife in Nigeria*, 2nd ed., 1911.
Latourette, Kenneth Scott, *A History of Christian Missions in China*,
    S.P.C.K., London, 1929.
Marsden, Kate, *On Sledge and Horseback to Outcast Siberian Lepers*, 1893.
—— *My Mission to Siberia: A vindication*, 1921.
—— see also, Johnson, Henry.
Mason, Kenneth, *Abode of Snow*, Rupert Hart-Davis, 1955.
North, Marianne, *Recollections of a Happy Life*, (ed. Mrs. John
    Addington Symonds), 2 vols., 1892.
—— *Further Recollections of a Happy Life*, 1893.
Pavey, Elizabeth, *The Story of the Growth of Nursing*, Faber and
    Faber, 1951.

Bibliography

Robinson, R., John Gallagher and Alice Denny, *Africa and the Victorians: the Official Mind of Imperialism*, Macmillan, 1961.

Robson, Isabella S., *Two Lady Missionaries in Tibet*, 1909.

Sawyer, Major H. A., *A Reconnaissance in the Bakhtiari Country, South-west Persia*, Simla: Government Central Printers, 1891.

Sheldon, May French, (translator):
Flaubert, Gustave, *Salammbo*, 1887.
—— *Herbert Severance*, 1889.
—— *Sultan to Sultan*, 1892.

Stoddart, Anna, *Life of Isabella Bird*, 1906.

Taylor, Annie R., 'Diary', *in* William Carey's *Travel and Adventure in Tibet*, 1902.
—— *see also*, Robson, I.S.

Taylor, Dr. and Mrs. Howard, *Life of Hudson Taylor*. 2 vols: *I. Growth of a Soul; II. Growth of a Work of God*, China Inland Mission, London, 1911.

Tweedie, Mrs. Alec, *Through Finland in Carts*, 1898.
—— *Thirteen Years of a Busy Life*, 1912.
—— *Women the World Over*, 1916.
—— *Me and Mine*, 1933.

Wallace, Kathleen, *This is your Home: A Portrait of Mary Kingsley*, Heineman, 1956.

Workman, Fanny Bullock and William Hunter:
—— *Algerian Memories*, 1895.
—— *Sketches Awheel in fin-de-siècle Iberia*, 1897.
—— *In the Ice World of the Himalaya*, 1900.
—— *Through Town and Jungle: 14,000 Miles Awheel among the Temples and Peoples of the Indian Plain*, 1904.
—— *Ice-bound Heights of the Mustagh*, 1908.
   Peaks and Glaciers of Nun Kun, 1909.
—— *The Call of the Snowy Hispar*, 1910.
—— *Two Summers in the Ice Wilds of the Eastern Karakoram*, 1917.

Younghusband, Francis, *India and Tibet*, 1910.

I have also read through and quoted from volumes of *The Queen* from 1888 onwards; back numbers of *China's Millions*, journal of the China Inland Mission, from 1884 to 1889; and individual numbers of *Womanhood* (November 1901), *The Lady's Gazette* (January 1902) and *The Temple Magazine* (September 1901), these last three containing articles by Alice Royle about May French Sheldon. Relevant volumes of the *Geographical Journal* have been consulted throughout, as have reports of the British Association for the Advancement of Science.

Index

Afghanistan, 42
Africa, East, 92, 93, 95, 96; *see also*
Sheldon, M. F., *passim and under
separate countries*
Africa, South, 6, 67, 68–9, 70, 176
Africa, West, 5, 7, 151, 152, 153,
171, 172, 173, 174; *see also*
Kingsley, M., *passim and under
separate countries*
Ainu, Hairy, aborigines of Japan,
5, 10, 38–9, 40
Ajumba tribe, 159, 160, 162
Albert, Lake, 94, 96
Alec-Tweedie, Mrs. E. B., 5, 9
Algeria, 76–7
America, North, 6, 10, 23, 57; *see
also* Bishop, I. B., *and* North,
Marianne, *passim*
Angola, 152
Armenians, 41
Austen, Col. H. H. Godwin, 81,
86
Australia, 6, 22, 64–5, 114; *see also*
North, M., *passim*

Baghdad, 40, 42, 43
Baker, Sir Samuel, 96
Bakhtiari country, 42, 46–7, 84
Bell, Gertrude, 3
Bird, Henrietta, 21, 23, 24, 28, 30,
33, 35, 36, 39, 41, 49
BISHOP, ISABELLA BIRD, **19–53**; 5, 6,
8, 10, 11, 14, 54, 57, 80, 81, 84,
124, 149, 150, 172
Bishop, Dr. John, 38, 39, 40, 49
Boer War, 176
Brazil, 57, 59–62, 67, 70, 108
Brooke, Rajah Charles and Mrs.,
63–5

British Assoc. for the Advancement
of Science, 9, 13, 48, 62, 103

Cable, Miss Mildred, 111
Calabar, 154, 155, 172
California, 62, 66–7, 71
Cameron, Julia, 64
Cameroon Mountain, 171–2
Canada, 6, 57, 62
Canton, 39, 109
Carey, William, 125–6
Ceylon, 64, 79, 82
Chala, Lake, 98–100, 103
Chamberlain, Joseph, 175
Chicago World Fair, 145
Chile, 69–70
China, 6, 23, 40, 41, 48, 49, 53, 109,
110, 111, 112, 119, 123; *see also*
Bishop, I. B., *and* Taylor, A.,
passim
China Inland Mission, 49, 108–14,
125, 131; see also Taylor, A.
Christie, Miss Ella, 10
Clothes, travellers' choice of, 4, 7, 8,
9, 19, 22, 25, 30, 49, 60, 63, 76,
85–6, 96, 98, 116, 124, 126, 135,
136, 139, 150, 152, 158, 161,
163–4, 172
Colenso, Bishop, 69
Colorado, 24, 35–8
'Comanche Bill', 32–3, 51
Congo, 6
——— Belgian, 103
——— Free State, 92, 152, 175
——— French, 97, 155; *see also for
Congo in general*, Kingsley, M.,
passim
Conway, Martin, 81, 83
Cooper, Thomas Thornville, 116

Index

Corisco, 169–70, 172
Crown Colony system, 174
Cumming, Miss C. Gordon, 4, 5, 19
Curzon, Lord, 13, 14
Cust, Miss M. *and* Mr. R. N., 12
Cycling, 7, 75, 76–80, 172

Darchendo, *see* K'ang-ting
Darjeeling, 80, 114, 116, 124, 126
Darwin, Charles, 55, 62, 65, 66
Davidson, Lilias Campbell, 7, 9
Denver, 30, 31, 32, 36
Duncan, Miss Jane Ellen, 6, 10, 15–16
Dowie, Miss Mené Muriel, 9
Dundas, Lady Christian (Sister Christian), 130, 131, 132

Edinburgh, 21, 53, 57
Emigration, Victorian belief in, 6
Estes Park, 25–31, 32, 33–7
Evangelical Deaconesses' Institute, 130, 131
Evangelical enthusiasm, 20–1, 107, 108, 130–1
Evans, Griffith, 27, 29, 30, 37, 38

Fan tribe, 157, 159, 160, 161–8, 169, 171, 173
Fernando Po, 154
Field, Miss Anna, 135, 138, 144
Fjort tribe, 152
Fleming, Peter, 113, 127
Food, choice of, 20, 37, 39, 40, 41, 47, 50, 53, 59, 63, 65, 66, 67, 77, 97, 113, 116, 117, 119, 120, 136, 142, 153, 159, 165, 166
Franklin, Lady, 10, 12
Franklin Search, 10, 12, 13

Gaboon, 159, 167, 170, 172
Galton, Sir Francis, 6, 55, 68
Germany, 56, 76, 77, 82, 94, 101, 102, 152, 171, 172
Goldie, Sir George, 81
Grant, General and family, 57–8
Gunther, Dr. 158, 176

Hatton and Cookson, 152, 155, 159, 168, 171
Hawaii (Sandwich Islands), 19, 21, 22–4, 40, 41, 48, 66
Himalaya, The, 3, 15, 64, 75, 76, 80–9; *see also* Workman, F. B. *passim*
Hong Kong, 39, 49, 109
Hooker, Sir Joseph, 55, 68
Huc, Abbé E. R., 107, 114, 116
Hwang-Ho, 113, 115, 117–18, 138

India, 10, 12, 20, 41, 42, 64, 70, 71, 76, 79–89, 125
—— Survey of, 80–1, 86, 87, 88
Imperial British East Africa Co., 95

Jamaica, 57–9, 62
Japan, 5, 10, 23, 38, 39, 40, 41, 49, 62, 63, 70
Java, 5, 63, 64, 82
Johnson, Henry, 128, 132, 133
Johnson, Captain (Obanjo), 168–9
Jyekundo (Kegu), 115, 119, 122, 123

Kansu, 112, 113
K'ang-ting (Darchendo, Ta-chien-lu), 52, 115, 119, 123
Karakoram range, 42, 76, 80, 83, 86, 87, 88; *see also* Workman, F. B., *passim*
Karun river, 43, 46–7
Kashmir, 41, 80, 81, 82–8
Kenya, 94, 98
Kew Gardens, 54, 55, 64, 68, 69, 70
Kick, Wilhelm, 86
Kilimanjaro, Mt., 8, 90, 94, 95, 98, 101
Kingsley, George, 150, 151
KINGSLEY, MARY, **149–76**; 4, 5, 6, 7, 8, 14, 15, 85, 97, 134
Koko Nor, 113
Kogan, Madame Claude, 86
Korea, 40, 41, 42, 48, 49
Kumbum Monastery, 113
Kurdistan, 41, 47–8

Index

Lanchow, 112, 113
Larymore, Mrs. Constance, 8
Laseron, Dr. Michael, 130
Le Blond, Mrs., 8
Lena river, 138
Leopold II, King, 97, 103, 151–2, 175
Leprosy, 23, 128, 132, 133, 134, 138–43, 144–5
Lhasa, 7, 52, 107, 114, 116, 119, 120, 121, 125, 127
Libreville, 155, 159
Liverpool, 7, 31, 152, 153, 154, 172, 175
Livingstone, David, 5, 6, 93, 107, 128, 150, 172
Long's Peak, 25, 26, 27, 28, 29, 34, 36
Longstaff, Dr. Tom, 81
Luristan, 42, 46–7

McClintock, Admiral Sir Leopold, 12–13
MacDonald, Sir Claude and Lady, 154
Mackenzie, George, 95, 102
Macmillan, George, 153, 172
MacRobert, Lady (Rachel Workman), 89
Magellan, Straits of, 69
Malaya, 21, 23, 39, 41
Manchuria, 49, 110
MARSDEN, KATE, 128–45; 5, 7, 14, 149
Masai tribe, 90, 94, 95, 98, 102
Mauna Loa volcano, 23, 29
Medicine, practice of by travellers, 47, 84, 92, 109, 113, 114, 165
Mekong river, 118, 123
Min river, 51
Missionary endeavour, 6, 23, 40, 41, 48, 49, 107–9, 123, 124; see Taylor, A., passim
Missions, French Protestant, 155, 156
Moffat, Dr. R., 108–9
Morocco, 53
Moscow, 133, 135, 144

Mountaineering, 7, 8, 9, 80, 81, 83, 86–7, 88, 89
Mukden, 49
Mull, Isle of, 6, 21, 24, 39, 48, 53
Murray, John, 8, 24, 38, 39, 49
Murray, Captain, 153

Ness, Mrs. Patrick, 13
Nestorian Christians, 41, 48
New Guinea, 39
New Zealand, 6, 22, 66, 108, 132, 145
Ngologs (Goloks) of Tibet, 118
Niagara Falls, 20, 57
Nigeria, 8
Nightingale, Florence, 12, 128, 129
Noga, 116–122
North, Frederick, 6, 55, 56, 67
NORTH, MARIANNE, 54–71; 4, 5, 6, 10, 14, 39, 172

Ogowé river, 149, 155, 158, 159, 161, 167, 171, 172, 173
Oil Rivers Protectorate, 154–5

Parke, Surgeon T. H., 93, 97
Peck, Miss Annie, 87
Penting, 117, 118, 119, 121, 122–3
Persia, 21, 35, 40, 41–8, 49, 80; see Bishop, I. B., passim
Photography, 4, 41, 50, 77, 80
Pontso, 114–25, 127
Prince of Wales's General Hospital, Tottenham, 130
Procopieff, Jean, 139
Punch, 14

The Queen, 9, 75, 109, 124, 130, 131

Rembwé river, 159, 160, 162, 165, 166, 167–9, 172
Rhins, Dutreuil de, 123
Rijnhart, Peter and Susie, 123
Rocky Mountains, 8, 20, 23, 24, 25, 31, 32, 33, 40, 41, 91; see Bishop, I. B., passim
'Rocky Mountain Jim' (Jim Nugent), 10, 23–38, 46

Index

Rowan, Mrs. Ellis, 65
Royal Geographical Society, 10–15, 68, 81, 88, 93, 108, 145, 164
Royal Scottish Geographical Society, 11
Rudolf, Lake, 98
Russia, 42, 43, 49, 80, 128, 131, 133–45; see Marsden, Kate, passim

Sandwich Isles, see Hawaii
San Francisco, 24, 63, 66
Sarawak, 63, 65
Sawyer, Major Herbert, 35, 42–7, 80
Schweitzer, Dr. Albert, 128, 155
'Scramble for Africa', 94, 151
Seychelles, 69
Shanghai, 109, 113, 114
Sheldon, Eli Lemon, 4, 92, 93, 94, 103
SHELDON, MAY FRENCH, 90–103; 4, 6, 7, 8, 14, 15
Siberia, 14, 49, 117, 134, 135, 136, 137, see also Marsden, K., passim
Sierra Leone, 174
Sikkim, 80, 114, 124, 125–7
Slessor, Mary, 155
Somerville, Mary, 11, 81
Spain, 77–9
Speke, John Hanning, 11
Spurgeon, Dr. C. H., 40, 54
Stairs, Captain W. G., 97
Stanhope, Lady Hester, 3
Stanley, Sir Henry Morton, 7, 92, 93, 97, 152
Stoddart, Anna, 53
Survey of India, see India
Symonds, Mrs Addington, 57, 70
Syria, 56
Szechwan, 15, 50, 81

Ta-chien-lu, see K'ang-ting
Tanganyika, 94, 102
Tangier, 78
Taveta, 94, 97, 98
TAYLOR, ANNIE R., 107–27; 6, 42, 131, 138
Taylor, Rev. James Hudson, 109–12, 113

Tehran, 40, 42, 43, 46
Teleki, Count Rudolf, 98
Tenerife, 62
Thomson, Joseph, 94, 97, 172
Tibet, 11, 15–16, 41, 42, 50, 51, 107, 112–27; see Taylor, A., passim
The Times, 8, 13, 25
Tinné, Alexine, 11
Tottenham, 130, 131
Turkey, 40, 41, 47–8, 56

United States, 26, 57, 62, 66, 67, 68, 70, 90; see also Bishop, I. B., and North, M., passim and under separate regional headings

Victoria, Lake, 94
Victoria, H.M. Queen, 3, 9, 11, 145
Viluisk (Siberia), 135, 139, 141, 144
Vinokouroff, Father John, 139, 141
Vladivostock, 49

Washington, 57
Wellcome, H. S., 92
Wellstead, James, 129
White House, The, 57–8
Wilberforce, W. (1759–1833), 20
Wolff, Sir Henry Drummond, 43, 46
Women, rights of, 3–4, 7, 46–7, 75, 77, 78, 88, 172
WORKMAN, FANNY BULLOCK, 75–89; 3, 6, 7, 14, 15, 90, 149
Workman, William Hunter, 4, 76–89

Yakut, 128, 139, 140–3
Yalung river, 51
Yangtze river, 41, 49, 50, 53, 110, 112, 118
Yatung, 42, 125, 126, 127
Yenissei river, 138
Younghusband, Sir Francis, 42, 81, 125

Zagros mountains, 42, 43
Zanzibar, 94, 95, 96, 102, 103